"As our culture collapses around us, the issues of bioethics lie at the heart of its  address the foundational every culture is premised what it means to be huma

"In this series these ext with due seriousness (they with accessibility (no one who thinks will be excluded). It is hard to imagine a more important set of questions or a more timely publication."

Nigel M. de S. Cameron, Ph.D.
Provost, Trinity International University

"These booklets are packed with information and moral insights that will provide needed help to pastors, health care professionals, and teachers seeking direction in the everchanging world of bioethics. Nothing less than human dignity hangs in the balance."

Francis J. Beckwith, Ph.D.
Associate Professor of Philosophy, Culture, and Law
Trinity Graduate School and Trinity Law School
Trinity International University

The BioBasics Series provides insightful and practical answers to many of today's pressing bioethical questions. Advances in medical technology have resulted in longer and healthier lives, but they have also produced interventions and procedures that call for serious ethical evaluation. What we can do is not necessarily what we should do. This series is designed to instill in each reader an uncompromising respect for human life that will serve as a compass through a maze of challenging questions.

This series is a project of The Center for Bioethics and Human Dignity, an international organization located just north of Chicago, Illinois, in the United States of America. The Center endeavors to bring Christian perspectives to bear on today's many difficult bioethical challenges. It develops book, audio tape, and video tape series; presents numerous conferences in different parts of the world; and offers a variety of other printed and computer-based resources. Through its membership program, the Center provides world-wide resources on bioethical matters. Members receive the Center's international journal, *Ethics and Medicine,* the Center's newsletter, *Dignity,* the Center's *Update Letters,* special World Wide Web access, an Internet News Service and Discussion Forum, and discounts on most bioethics resources in print.

For more information on membership in the Center or its various resources, including present or future books in the BioBasics Series, contact the Center at:

The Center for Bioethics and Human Dignity
2065 Half Day Road
Bannockburn, IL 60015 USA
Phone: (847) 317-8180 Fax: (847) 317-8153
E-mail: cbhd@banninst.edu

Information and ordering is also available through the Center's World Wide Web site on the Internet: http://www.bioethix.org

BioBasics Series

Basic Questions on

Alternative Medicine

What Is Good and What Is Not?

Gary P. Stewart, D.Min.
William R. Cutrer, M.D.
Timothy J. Demy, Th.D.
Dónal P. O'Mathúna, Ph.D.
Paige C. Cunningham, J.D.
John F. Kilner, Ph.D.
Linda K. Bevington, M. A.

kregel
PUBLICATIONS

Grand Rapids, MI 49501

Basic Questions on Alternative Medicine: What Is Good and What Is Not?

Published by Kregel Publications, a division of Kregel, Inc., P.O. Box 2607, Grand Rapids, MI 49501. Kregel Publications provides trusted, biblical publications for Christian growth and service. Your comments and suggestions are valued.

Scripture quotations are from the *New American Standard Bible*, © the Lockman Foundation 1960, 1962, 1963, 1968, 1971, 1972, 1973, 1975, 1977.

Some Scripture quotations are from the *Holy Bible: New International Version®*. Copyright © 1973, 1978, 1984 by International Bible Society. Used by permission of Zondervan Publishing House. All rights reserved.

Cover and book design: Nicholas G. Richardson

ISBN 0-8254-3071-2

Printed in the United States of America

3 4 5 / 02 01 00 99

Table of Contents

Spirituality and Alternative Therapies

Contributors

Linda K. Bevington, M.A., is the Project Manager for the Center for Bioethics and Human Dignity, Bannockburn, Illinois.

Paige C. Cunningham, J.D., has written numerous articles on abortion and the law; she is a coauthor of the amicus brief that Justice O'Connor cited in her discussion of viability in *Webster v. Reproductive Health Services.*

William R. Cutrer, M.D., served for many years as an obstetrician/gynecologist specializing in the treatment of infertility. He is currently serving as the Dallas/Fort Worth Area Director for The Christian Medical and Dental Society.

Timothy J. Demy, Th.M., Th.D., is a military chaplain and coauthor and author of numerous books and articles. He is a member of the Evangelical Theological Society.

John F. Kilner, Ph.D., is Director of the Center for Bioethics and Human Dignity, Bannockburn, Illinois. He is also Professor of Bioethics and Contemporary Culture at Trinity International University, Deerfield, Illinois.

Dónal P. O'Mathúna, Ph.D., is Associate Professor of Medical Ethics and Chemistry at Mount Carmel College of Nursing, Columbus, Ohio.

Gary P. Stewart, Th.M., D.Min., is a military chaplain and coauthor of numerous books and articles. He is a member of the Evangelical Theological Society.

Introduction

Alternative therapies are receiving much attention today. News magazines regularly carry the topic as their cover stories. Books on alternative therapies by physicians such as Andrew Weil, Deepak Chopra, Herbert Benson, and Larry Dossey regularly make the best-seller lists. Medical and nursing schools are adding courses in alternative therapies. Hospitals are thinking about providing them, insurance companies are covering them, and state-run insurance programs are mandating coverage for specific therapies. As much as $40 billion is spent annually on alternative therapies in the United States.[1]

The growing interest in alternative therapies is not difficult to understand. People sometimes turn to alternative therapies after a negative or unsatisfying experience with the way the modern health-care system provides "care." Physicians often have little time to spend with their patients, many of whom they barely know. Patients feel shuffled in and out of offices, hooked up to one instrument after another, poked and prodded for unknown reasons, and finally handed a huge bill. They often come away from an impersonal medical business feeling confused, not really heard, and even scared.

While certainly a generalization, this characterizes the experiences of many. TV shows and commercials portray hospitals and physicians as having the power to cure almost everything. Meanwhile, individuals experience the tragic reality that modern health care has limitations and problems. We know we can't live forever, but somehow we got the idea that medicine will, in the end, save us. When people realize that it can't, they often feel abandoned by the system they thought would rescue them.

Into this environment comes an "alternative"—a way to approach health and healing that is personal and caring. Practitioners of alternative therapies spend lots of time going over every aspect of a patient's life. They don't rush from one appointment to the next and seem genuinely interested in each patient. Insurance might not cover the costs, but the charges seem reasonable and all that annoying paperwork is eliminated! Unlike much of conventional medicine, alternative therapists don't compare their practices to a war against disease. Rather, they focus on building up each person in order to ward off disease. In so doing, they focus on the person rather than the disease. Therefore, the turn to alternative therapies is partly a reaction against a system perceived as impersonal, financially driven, and lacking in humility. Certainly, many within conventional medicine are caring professionals focused on doing their best for their patients. But confidence in the system as a whole is decreasing, and people are becoming more open to considering alternatives.

People should indeed pursue the therapies that are the most effective and affordable. They need not assume that conventional medicine is always the safest and most effective answer to curing human ills. But they must also be discerning. This book will divide alternative therapies into five categories so that each can be evaluated on its own merits. It serves as a map to help bring people through the mountains and valleys of alternative medicine safely so that choices about one's care can be made with confidence. There are aspects of alternative therapies that we can welcome and promote, other aspects we must remain uncertain about, and still others we must completely reject.

This book is not intended to reproduce all the available information on the subject but rather to simplify, complement, and supplement other available sources that the reader is encouraged to consult. Some of these materials have been listed at the end of this book. This book is not intended to take the place of theological, legal, medical, or psychological counsel or treatment. If assistance in any of these areas is needed, please seek the services of a certified professional. The views expressed in this work are solely those of the authors and do not represent or reflect the position or endorsement of any governmental agency or department, military or otherwise.

1. What is health?

Some see health as the absence of disease or pain. This view is criticized by proponents of alternative therapies as too narrow. In contrast, the World Health Organization defines health very broadly. "Health is a state of complete physical, mental and social well-being and not merely the absence of disease or infirmity. The enjoyment of the highest attainable standard of health is one of the fundamental rights of every human being without distinction of race, religion, political belief, economic or social condition."[2] While this definition has been criticized as unattainable, it captures important aspects of health also affirmed by the Bible. A biblical view of health includes physical, mental, and social well-being but also adds the spiritual dimension. God's will is for people to have "good health, just as your soul prospers" (3 John 2). Many alternative therapies would agree with the inclusion of spiritual well-being. However, the Bible maintains that spiritual well-being, an essential ingredient for the "abundant life," is only attainable through a personal relationship with Jesus Christ (John 10:10).

The Hebrew term for healing, *rapa'*, was used to describe the repairing of a broken jar, the healing of a person, and the restoring of the nation of Israel. The fundamental meaning of the word, then, is to restore something to its original condition, or make it whole again.[3] God's activity as Healer is not separated into physical and spiritual realms, but refers to His work in every aspect of people's lives. This holistic view of health is present also in the New Testament, especially in words for healing such as *sozo* ("salvation"), meaning the complete restoration or healing of a believer's body, soul, and spirit (Mark 10:52; Luke 8:48).

Many things contribute to good health: a proper diet, exercise, sleep, stress reduction, and good relationships with other people and God. Common sense, along with a growing body of research evidence, shows that these are important for healthier lifestyles and the prevention of various illnesses. Many alternative therapies are attractive because they address these areas of people's lives. But they are not necessarily incompatible with conventional medicine; in fact, proper diet and behavior have traditionally been seen as part of what any good physician would recommend to his or her patients.

One of the most enduring images of healing is that of the Good Samaritan (Luke 10:30–37). The Samaritan went out of his way to help meet the physical and other needs of a complete stranger whom he found injured beside the road. Those who recognize that all people are created in the image of God have historically offered and should continue to offer care and compassion to those in need of healing in this hurting world. Helping people meet their physical, spiritual, and relational needs is central to the mission of the Church.

The most important, yet often the most neglected, aspect of good health is a person's spiritual well-being. Scripture, unlike conventional or alternative medicine, claims that good health depends on dealing with moral guilt (Ps. 32:3–4; 1 Cor. 11:29–30). Throughout the Old Testament, poor health is associated with sin (2 Chron. 21:18–19; Ps. 41:4), while good health is a manifestation of God's mercy and love (Gen. 20:17). However, Jesus makes it clear that specific illnesses are not always caused by an individual's sin (Luke 13:1–5; John

9:1–3). Instead, illness and poor health are generally the natural consequences of living in a fallen world (Gen. 2:17; Job 1–2, 42; Rom. 5:12–21). Accepting the truth of the death, burial, and resurrection of Jesus Christ and living an obedient faith produces a spiritual healing that reduces much of the behavior that can cause illness and even an early death. He is the ultimate source of healing (John 6:35–40). Good relationships with other people also matter. Not only a life lived in intimate relationship with Jesus Christ, but also one lived in fellowship with others and in service of others, is essential for good health (John 10:10; Acts 20:35).

2. Who is responsible for your health?

Western society places great emphasis on personal freedom—sometimes calling it "autonomy" (or self-rule). Ideally, patients have the final say in the therapies and procedures they use. However, there is also a long tradition of paternalism, that is, "doctor knows best." Patients have tended to trust whatever their physicians recommend because of physicians' greater knowledge and experience. This century's scientific developments, of which medicine is a part, have improved public health and sanitation. New technology and drugs have led to complicated medical practices that only trained physicians seem able to understand.

However, a negative side-effect of these developments has been the belief that health and illness are purely physical in nature. The importance of other influences on health, such as diet, exercise, emotions, and spirituality has been neglected. We think that we can live life as we want and the physician can fix any problems that result. The technological advances in medical intervention and the technical abilities of the physician have distorted the role of medicine. Some have viewed medicine as humanity's savior. In the process, individual responsibility for health has been overlooked.

Since the 1960s, however, people have become more likely to question the authority of those in the medical profession. Personal freedom has become more important. People want to take more responsibility for their health. They want to know what physicians are doing to them and why new technology seems to cause as many problems as it resolves. Overall, people's trust in physicians has waned.

However, the pendulum has swung all the way from regarding the physician as god to seeing the patient as god. Personal autonomy now dominates modern medicine. Abortion and euthanasia are justified by people who believe that they have the right to do with their bodies whatever they wish. Similarly, those who want alternative therapies say they are entitled to use whatever therapeutic option is available, even if others think it is strange or ineffective. Therefore, the responsibility for health care is placed solely on patients' shoulders—health-care professionals become little more than counselors and providers of the services patients want.

The biblical view of responsibility for health is God-centered rather than self-centered. Our bodies are gifts (or better, loans) from God for which we are responsible to care—they have been purchased by the blood of Christ. They are not our own to do with as we please. Instead, by faith, we should pursue good health to glorify God, serve others (Rom. 14:7–8; 1 Cor. 6:19–20; 2 Cor. 5:15; Phil. 1:20–26), and participate in everything that God has given us to enjoy (1 Tim. 6:17). Only in this context will believers be able to experience the abundant life Christ has offered (John 10:10).

Although health is ultimately from God (Ps. 103:1–5), each individual bears a great responsibility for his or her own health. However, health care should be a partnership among health-care professionals, the patient, and the family or close friends and relatives. Absolute autonomy brings isolation, while faith in God and association with others provide companionship, confidence, and comfort. When considering alternative medicine, it would be wise to seek guidance not only from a physician whom you trust but also from members of the church whom you believe possess gifts of knowledge, wisdom, discernment, and counseling. Responsibility for health can be shared when people of the church use their gifts for the good of others (Rom. 12:3–8; 1 Cor. 12:7, 12–26; Eph. 4:11–16; 1 Peter 4:7–11).

3. What is alternative medicine?

An initial challenge to understanding alternative medicine or therapies is defining what is being discussed. Many different terms are used to describe the treatments involved, such as alternative, complementary, unorthodox, unconventional, unproven, holistic, fringe, integrative, natural, or New Age therapies or medicine. The term *alternative therapies* will be used here because it remains the most popular term, although the term *complementary therapies* is growing in popularity. In contrast to these therapies are those known as conventional, modern, scientific, orthodox, allopathic, reductionistic, biochemical, or physicalistic. The terms *conventional therapies* and *conventional medicine* will be used when referring to this group of therapies.

The defining characteristics of each group can be described in various ways. Conventional therapies are often defined as those associated with physicians and hospitals. This definition has the advantage of identifying who provides which type of therapy, but the distinctions are not as clear-cut as they once were. Many prestigious medical centers now have alternative medicine departments, and nurses in particular are increasingly interested in providing alternative therapies.

Another common distinction between the two groups is that alternative therapies tend to have little or no clinical research to support their safety or effectiveness in contrast to the therapies of conventional medicine. However, some providers of alternative therapies note that some conventional medical practices also have not been rigorously tested. Moreover, a few alternative therapies are now undergoing testing. So while evidence of any therapy's safety and effectiveness is vital, this does not appear to be a definitive distinguishing characteristic.

Any definition of alternative therapies will tend to be either too broad or too narrow. Broad definitions are more typical. For example, physical therapy, counseling, nutrition, and massage are listed as the alternative therapies used most frequently by people with multiple sclerosis.[4] Those most commonly covered by HMOs are chiropractic, weight-loss programs, acupuncture, relaxation therapy, mental imagery, massage, and hypnosis.[5] Another study included active listening and patient advocacy as natural therapies.[6] Few would deny the importance of these factors in promoting and maintaining health; but by listing them as alternative therapies, the popularity of alternative therapies as a whole appears greater than may actually be the case. Also, the impression is conveyed that conventional medicine does not value such concerns as weight loss and patient advocacy as highly as does alternative medicine—which may not be true.

Instead of lumping all alternative therapies into one group, we will divide them into five categories.[7] Some of the therapies have much to offer patients and should be encouraged, some should be rejected completely, and others fall somewhere in between.

Complementary therapies—therapies such as diet, exercise, and stress reduction that address broader lifestyle issues.

Scientifically unproven therapies—therapies, such as many herbal remedies, with a foundation in established medical and scientific principles but for which very little scientific evidence exists.

Scientifically questionable therapies—therapies, such as homeopathy, based on principles that contradict well-established scientific principles or that cannot be easily verified.

Life-energy therapies—therapies, such as therapeutic touch or Reiki, that assume the existence of "life energy" that can be manipulated by a variety of techniques.

Quackery and fraud—therapies that have been shown to have no reasonable benefit but that are still promoted by committed adherents. Fraud can occur with any therapy but especially with alternative therapies because they usually lack adequate research and rely on patient testimonials for validation.

While any classification scheme is somewhat arbitrary—therapies will move from one category to another based on new information—classification has advantages. We need not accept or reject alternative therapies as a whole, but we can evaluate each therapy based on the category or categories to which it belongs. Complementary therapies generally seem to play an important role in promoting health, whereas quackery should always be exposed and rejected. Christians should reject, on theological grounds, therapies based on life energy. Decisions about *scientifically unproven therapies* and *scientifically questionable therapies* will have to be made case-by-case with reliance on the best scientific evidence available.

4. Will my health insurance pay for alternative therapies?

Health insurance companies are increasingly paying for alternative therapies. One survey found that 58 percent of health maintenance organizations (HMOs) had already planned to cover alternative therapies by 1998.[8] Oxford Health Plans unveiled the first alternative therapies program as an add-on to conventional insurance in 1997. Some states mandate coverage for specified alternative therapies on state-run programs. However, this does not mean that all therapies will be covered. A 1995 survey found that 86 percent of HMOs covered chiropractic; 69 percent, weight-loss programs; 31 percent, acupuncture; and 28 percent, relaxation therapy.[9] This survey also found that 31 percent of HMOs discourage use of herbal remedies, 24 percent discourage acupuncture and hypnosis, and 14 percent discourage mental-imagery therapy. Insurance covers alternative therapies but usually those most similar to conventional therapies.

Insurance interest in alternative therapies is primarily economic. All parties involved in the health-care industry are seeking more effective ways to use limited resources. Alternative therapies focus on prevention of illness—which is viewed as a legitimate way to reduce costs (although whether preventive care actually reduces overall costs is disputed). Alternative therapies are usually less expensive than conventional therapies. For example, treatment of an enlarged prostate will cost about $8 a month with the saw palmetto herb, but $50 to $75 a month with the pharmaceutical finasteride.[10] While efforts to reduce costs can be legitimate, great effort must be exerted to ensure that results are not compromised. One of the dangers is that financial pressures will encourage the coverage and use of less expensive, but ineffective, alternative therapies instead of effective, but more expensive, conventional therapies.

Insurance companies are covering alternative therapies because of patient demand. A spokesman for the Health Insurance Association of America stated: "The decision to cover is made by the purchaser, not the seller. . . . After all, insurers are in the business of selling coverage, and they respond to market demand."[11] But choosing therapies is not the same as choosing clothing styles. The consequences are much more serious, and the knowledge level needed is much higher. For this reason, decisions about therapies and their coverage should be based on their safety and effectiveness, not their popularity. But given our society's adoration of autonomy, it is likely that more insurance companies will cover alternative therapies even before their effectiveness is fully documented.

EVALUATING ALTERNATIVE THERAPIES

5. What are the core guiding principles for selecting alternative therapies?

Choosing whether or not to use an alternative therapy can be a complicated and confusing task. No book on alternative therapies will ever be complete because new therapies are introduced regularly. To help you make decisions, four general guiding principles are provided here.

Realism. Fitness, health, and beauty have been pursued passionately by baby boomers. Yet this generation is still aging and getting ill. The "perfect health" and "ageless bodies" promoted by one of alternative medicine's main gurus, Deepak Chopra, resonate well with those who have worshiped personal health and fitness. W. Brugh Joy declares in his energy healing book, *Joy's Way,* that when we recognize the power of belief *"we can create anything we desire,"* including good health.

But some chronic illnesses cannot be cured, only controlled. Eventually, most of us who are able to avoid death by injury will some day die of a terminal illness. Alternative therapies are most commonly used to treat chronic and terminal conditions for which conventional medicine can do very little. The persistent search for a cure can sometimes become a way to deny the inevitable. At some point, people may have to accept that a cure for their condition does not exist. This acceptance can be very difficult for all involved and calls for great sensitivity. However, coming to terms with the reality of one's mortality is important.

As Christians, we, too, can get caught up in the search for personal health and comfort. There is nothing inherently wrong with this search as long as the therapies we choose restore, improve, or maintain our life or health, i.e., they truly have benefit. But the reality is that we live in fallen bodies that, with the passing of time, groan along with the rest of creation (Ps. 90:9–10; Rom. 8:18–23). Our present and eternal hope should be in the certainty of God's love for us (Rom. 8:35–39) and His prophetic promises, not in the exaggerated claims of miracle cures, wonder drugs, and promoters of "ageless bodies." In choosing any treatment, we must ensure that our goals and the claims of any therapy are realistic.

Stewardship. In matters of health and healing, we should exercise stewardship of our resources. Our lives and bodies are resources with which we can serve and glorify God (Rom. 14:7–8; 1 Cor. 6:19–20). We can use these resources wisely by maintaining our health through proper diet, exercise, relaxation, ministry, and spiritual nourishment. Prayer and wise counsel will help us balance these. Just as we consider how much we spend on our food and homes, we must question whether the money we spend on our health, whether for conventional or alternative therapies, represents good stewardship of our personal and societal resources.

Stewardship requires us to ask how effective a therapy is likely to be. Controlled studies best determine the effectiveness of any therapy. Using therapies demonstrated to be ineffective is a waste of monetary resources, which God tells us to manage wisely and effectively. Whether the therapy is a surgery, a high-tech instrument, an herb, or some energy-field manipulation makes no difference. Today's health-care resources are limited, and we must be careful not to waste them.

Harm. Therapies, however, can be worse than ineffective—they can be harmful. Many alternative therapies are assumed to be harmless because they are natural while drugs or surgery are not. But many pharmaceutical drugs were originally derived from herbs. Moreover, natural does not imply harmless. Tobacco products illustrate this point. Fatalities from herbal remedies occur every year, and complications from interactions between herbal remedies and other medicines are a growing problem.

Other alternative therapies that do not involve the ingestion of products can also cause harm. There is growing evidence that meditation causes emotional and psychological problems in many practitioners (see question 23). Proponents of therapeutic touch admit that harm can be caused by "energy overload," especially with very young, very old, or debilitated patients (see question 29). There is also indirect harm from using ineffective treatments if the available benefits of well-proven therapies are missed as a result. The documented potential harms and benefits of any alternative therapy should be investigated before trying it. If there is no documentation of this sort, it is usually wise to avoid that therapy.

Spiritual Issues. For Christians and non-Christians alike, the most serious potential harm caused by alternative therapies is spiritual. Many forms of alternative medicine claim that physical healing is based on the manipulation of a nonphysical human energy field, one that cannot be detected by physical instruments. This energy goes by various names, such as life energy, chi, prana, or Ki (see question 36), and underlies therapeutic touch, applied kinesiology, reflexology, pulse diagnosis, and others (see questions 17 and 29). Belief in its existence is deeply rooted in Eastern mystical religions and Western occult traditions. The increased acceptance of holistic healing, illustrated by these therapies, is the cultural trend most admired by *New Age Journal*.

Unfortunately, some Christians view this life energy as the power of God and dive headlong into therapies that utilize it. We must avoid calling something God's power when we are not certain of its origin. We cannot accept the belief that God reveals Himself as anything people want Him to be. Truth about God is not personally or culturally derived but emanates (or flows) from the character and will of the sovereign God. We must evaluate each therapy in light of its claims and then see if it is actually from God (1 John 4:1–3). Proponents of some alternative therapies, such as Reiki (see question 26), openly admit that their life-energy methods originate in occult practices. Others are thinly disguised versions of occult healing rituals. Even if these therapies do heal, Christians must be willing to forgo them. Physical health should not be sought at the expense of spiritual health (Mark 9:43–48).

6. How can I know if the claims for therapies are accurate and reliable?

Proving the cause of any change in health (either for the better or for the worse) is very difficult. Accordingly, a new drug must go through extensive and expensive testing before being released for widespread use. Pharmaceutical companies must demonstrate that new drugs are both effective and safe. Products usually go through *in vitro* tests (done on cells in a lab), animal testing, and, finally, clinical studies. The latter involve humans, starting with small numbers of healthy volunteers and eventually, if the drug proves to be safe, involving large numbers of ill patients.

However, it is well known that many improvements result from patients' believing in a treatment or trusting the person administering it, regardless of whether it actually works or not. This is called the placebo effect. A placebo is a pill or therapy that has no known physiological effects in and of itself. Sugar pills are the best-known placebos. In testing the effectiveness of a new instrument, a placebo might involve hooking someone up to a similar-looking device that actually does nothing. In this way, researchers can measure the effects of the new instrument on patients against the effects of the placebo instrument on other patients. It is commonly believed that 30 percent of patients will get better no matter what treatment they are given (due to the placebo effect). However, studies have found that up to 100 percent of patients given certain placebos show improvements.[12]

In practice, the placebo effect is an important contributor to healing. Practitioners, whether conventional or alternative, are assured of helping some patients no matter what they give them. However, when trying to determine if a therapy works or doesn't (and thus if it is worth an investment of time and money), the role of the placebo effect must be established. Clinical studies do this by giving some participants the therapy and giving others a placebo. The two groups of participants are then treated in exactly the same way. Those given the placebo form the control group. Those given the actual treatment form the test group.

To ensure that the experimental groups are as similar to each other as possible, two important steps are taken. First, people are randomly assigned to a group. If participants in the experiment could choose their own groups, those confident in the effectiveness of most therapies might choose to be in the test group, while those more suspicious of therapies might choose to be in the control group. This type of involvement by the participants would corrupt the results of the experiment and, therefore, result in a misrepresentation of the actual therapeutic value of the therapy being tested. Second, the two groups must be large enough to ensure they are as similar as possible. Statistical methods help determine the appropriate size of the groups.

Finally, researchers must ensure that they don't inadvertently influence people's recovery. Studies have shown that patients improve more when the practitioners believe in the therapy. Therefore, careful procedures are followed to ensure that neither the participants nor the researchers know who receives the test therapy and who receives the placebo. This double-blind method of research protects the integrity of the study, i.e., it limits unnecessary influences so that the results of the experiment are more likely to be associated with the therapy being tested.

Before calling something a cure (and selling it as such), it must be tested. Please take the time to examine closely the studies cited to support a therapy. Randomized, double-blind clinical trials give more reliable (though not infallible) data. Claims supported only by testimonials or surveys should be read critically and cautiously (see also questions 8 and 9).

7. What is "junk science"?

Junk science, or pseudoscience, is used to describe claims alleging scientific support that closer examination reveals not to be true. Those who use junk science either do not uphold the usual scientific standards of evidence, misinterpret the findings, or are dogmatic about controversial issues within science. Since the term is used to discredit scientific-sounding claims, labeling something as junk science is controversial and often contentious. The scientific method is a general way to approach problems, not a step-by-step process agreed upon by all scientists. Its core distinguishing characteristic is an emphasis on reproducible experiments to validate the claims being made.

In spite of the difficulty in determining what constitutes good science, and thereby what constitutes junk science, some guidelines must be established. Courts, including the United States Supreme Court, have called for clearer guidelines because of the increasingly important role played by scientific evidence in court rulings on such issues as tobacco-related illnesses, environmental hazards, and breast implants. Individuals also need guidelines to determine whether an alternative therapy's claims are based on junk science or good science. Health-care decisions should be based on only the most reliable evidence available.

Table 7–1 lists some characteristics to keep in mind when examining claims said to be scientifically supported. Final decisions should be based on a number of criteria. Give much less weight to claims from the junk-science categories than those supported by good science.

Table 7–1

Junk Science	Good Science
Claims are supported only by testimonials and endorsements	Claims are supported by controlled, double-blind studies (see question 6)
Studies conducted by people with unfamiliar credentials at institutions you have never heard of	Studies conducted by people with recognizable credentials (like M.D., Ph.D., Nobel Prize winner) at respected institutions
Studies published in journals you never heard of, often with esoteric names	Studies published in well-known, peer-reviewed journals
Therapies endorsed by movie stars or celebrities	Therapies endorsed by respected scientists who work in an area relevant to the claim

Claims appeal to vanity ("You know best!") or fear ("What if you don't try this?")	Claims appeal to the evidence
Therapy called a miracle cure or the latest breakthrough to revolutionize the field	Claims focus on the results and the evidence
Claims are unrealistic (guaranteed to cure, heals all known ailments)	Claims are realistic, acknowledging percent improvements and limitations
No claims are actually made (reports only ask questions)	Clear, specific claims are made and evidence given
Claims are made about pharmaceutical–medical conspiracies and persecution	Acknowledges and seeks to correct problems with the pharmaceutical–medical establishment

8. If it worked for someone else, should I try it?

We often try new things because someone told us about them. Whether it's a new restaurant, a mechanic, or a book, we are willing to try something because of someone's positive experience with it (called anecdotal evidence). But decisions to try a therapy should not be made the same way we decide on a restaurant. The consequences of mistakes with therapies far outweigh those with restaurants.

A problem with stories, anecdotes, and testimonials is that they only describe how people *felt* after a therapy. Much confusion could be removed if alternative therapists were more clear about whether they were simply helping people feel better or actually attempting to cure illnesses. Conventional practitioners, however, could learn much from alternative therapists about how to help people feel better while curing their diseases.

Another problem is that when we start to feel better, we often think the therapy we tried most recently caused that improvement. However, our bodies are amazingly complex and many factors affect our health and healing. Spontaneous remissions occur where an illness inexplicably disappears. For example, one in 100,000 cancers unexpectedly goes into remission no matter what therapies are attempted. Other illnesses will be overcome by the body's natural defenses. (The statement "If you take an aspirin for a cold it will be gone in a week; take nothing and it will be gone in seven days" reflects this reality.) Some chronic illnesses are cyclic where improvements are part of the natural progression of the disease. Factors such as diet, stress, and exercise play a role in health and healing, and the role of the mind in influencing recovery is only just beginning to be explored (see question 6). All of these factors complicate efforts to determine whether a therapy actually works or not.

Christians must also use God's Word to evaluate what they are being invited to try. Even when a therapy may appear harmless, it still may not be the appropriate course of action. Eve had a positive experience with the fruit in the Garden of Eden, but God held Adam accountable for not evaluating her invitation in light of His commands (Gen. 3:17). What could have been more harmless than for Saul to offer a sacrifice to God to ease his people's fear of the Philistines (1 Sam. 13:7–14)? The problem was that Saul was not authorized to offer this sacrifice; it was the responsibility of Samuel the high priest (1 Sam. 10:8). Although his action had a good intention, it cost his descendants the throne of Israel (see also Saul's consultation with a spirit medium in 1 Sam. 28:1–25). Scripture also requires a careful investigation of sweeping claims by an individual. For example, the Samaritan woman had a positive experience with Jesus at the well and invited others to hear Him (John 4). They did not just accept the woman's word, but examined what Jesus had to say (v. 42).

Christians must test the spirits of any spiritually based alternative therapy before participating in it (1 John 4:1–3). They must also examine the practitioner's belief system. Even if something works, it may be illegitimate for believers to use. Great signs and wonders can be performed by the power of Satan (Matt. 24:24; 2 Thess. 2:7–12). A subtle way to induce people to pursue spiritism and the occult is by speaking about the potential for healing. This is the case with some, but certainly not all, alternative therapies.

When someone tells you some therapy worked for him or her, your curiosity may be aroused. Please inquire further. Look for high-quality evidence that supports the therapeutic claims made for the therapy. Examine also the beliefs and worldview promoted by the therapy and its practitioners. Anecdotes encourage decision making based on experience alone, but these do not guarantee effectiveness or determine whether or not a particular approach is acceptable to God. Stories and testimonials make compelling reading, but they testify more to the versatility of the human mind and body than to a therapy's safety and effectiveness.

9. Is there a profit motive related to the acceptance or rejection of alternative therapies?

Promoters of alternative therapies frequently allege that their therapies are opposed by physicians and pharmaceutical companies out of fear of losing money. Conventional medicine does have a vested interest in retaining its share of health-care profits. However, there are other reasons that conventional therapies may be preferable to alternative options. Unlike many alternative therapies, many conventional therapies have demonstrated effectiveness. Patients regularly come to physicians after using ineffective alternative therapies only to discover that it is too late for conventional therapies that earlier could have helped significantly. The spiritual dangers of some alternative therapies explains why some physicians resist their use.

Some physicians and pharmaceutical companies are financially motivated to defend their methods. So, too, are some in the alternative-therapies business, which now generates up to $40 billion a year.[13] Americans spend $6 billion annually on nutritional supplements, and the market is growing by 20 percent every year.[14] Herbal and homeopathic products are not tested or regulated, making it much easier to sell low-quality products, thus increasing profits. Conventional therapies must demonstrate their effectiveness before being sold (and therefore before anyone can make a profit from them).

The popularity of alternative therapies has aroused the interest of managed-care organizations. The manager of the first alternative medicine program offered by a major health insurer (Oxford Health Plans) stated: "I believe that if the competitors don't listen to what their customers are saying and enter this [alternative medicine] market, they are going to lose a lot of business, and I'm going to take it from them."[15] Some physicians are mixing alternative and conventional therapies (called integrated medicine) to break away from financial dependence on health insurance altogether. An article in a mainstream medical journal makes the motive clear: "'Integrated Medicine' Could Boost Your Income."[16]

Decisions about whether to offer one therapy or another should be motivated by the desire to provide the best therapy with the fewest risks at the most reasonable cost. However, some practitioners will recommend therapies based on their potential for personal profit. This can occur with conventional or alternative therapies. Profiteering does not originate in the nature of the therapy but in people's fallen natures (Rom. 3:10–18). That is why we must insist on trustworthy evidence of effectiveness before expending resources on any therapy.

10. How are alternative therapies and practitioners regulated?

Laws and regulations are designed to root out quackery and fraud, which is laudable. Three federal agencies and the attorney general in each state have authority to prosecute quackery and fraud. Each state's attorney general has authority over the marketing of products and services within that state. The United States Postal Service enforces legislation requiring accuracy in the representation of products sold or distributed through the mail. The Federal Trade Commission regulates advertising practices, including those related to health care products and services. The Food and Drug Administration has the most extensive regulations dealing with the safety, effectiveness, and labeling of health care products and devices (see next question).

Conventional practitioners (like physicians, nurses, and physical therapists) are required to pass licensing examinations. Many alternative practitioners are not licensed. Much debate continues among alternative therapists concerning the value of licensing. Some see licensure as restrictive and power-focused. However, advocates see licensing as an important way to protect society from unscrupulous or poorly-prepared practitioners. For example, the American Association of Naturopathic Physicians works to regulate naturopathy (see question 24), believing that: "Licensure creates an infrastructure of accountability supported by law for the benefit of the people by affirming that the persons who possess the license are under the scrutiny of a board of examiners whose purpose is to protect the public by maintaining professional standards."[17]

However, many alternative therapies remain completely unregulated. Before visiting an alternative practitioner, do some background investigation. Find out what regulations in your state govern that therapy, and whether the practitioner has the necessary qualifications and appropriate professional affiliations. Ask about the training of the practitioner, and where it was conducted. Just like you would want to be sure that a physician really went to medical school, and that he or she practices according to professional standards, you should make sure an alternative therapist has adequate training and practices appropriately.

11. What is the role of the Food and Drug Administration (FDA) in alternative therapies?

The FDA enforces laws passed by Congress which apply to foods and/or drugs. When manufacturers claim that a product has therapeutic, curative or preventive value, it is then considered a drug. Hence, the labeling of drugs and products falls under the FDA's jurisdiction. New products in the United States must meet the most stringent standards in the world for safety and effectiveness. A number of hurdles must be overcome, such as animal testing and various types of human clinical trials to determine if a product can meet these standards and, if so, to identify the optimal dosage. This research and testing can take ten years and $300 million dollars. Once completed, the results are submitted to the FDA for review, which normally takes another year.

FDA standards of safety and efficacy are exceedingly difficult to meet, and the manufacturer carries a heavy burden of proof. One of the criticisms of this process is that only products which are patentable and potentially profitable make the application process worthwhile. Mere cost often bars innovations by individual practitioners from FDA review and approval. Consequently, only pharmaceutical drugs or unique processes developed by major pharmaceutical companies are worth submission to the FDA process.

One should not forget the example of thalidomide, a drug used by pregnant women in Europe during the 1960s which caused many severe birth defects. Stricter FDA regulations prevented thalidomide from going on the market in the United States before these problems were detected. Nevertheless, people struggle to find a balance between strict regulation and patients' needs, as is occurring with new fast-track approval for drugs designed for life-threatening diseases, such as AIDS. Different approval processes for therapies researched in other countries have caused some to question the slow regulatory process of the FDA and to seek reform. If the European Union harmonizes its pharmaceutical standards and practices, this may encourage the United States Congress and the FDA to rethink current policy on the review and approval of new drugs.

The FDA also regulates non-prescription dietary supplements under the Dietary Supplement Health and

Education Act (DSHEA) of 1994. The most common dietary supplements are vitamins, minerals, herbs, and amino acids. If labels make no therapeutic or curative claims, the product is not considered a drug. Manufacturers are not required to demonstrate that dietary supplements are safe or effective. The burden of proving safety is shifted from manufacturers to the FDA which cannot object to the selling of a supplement unless it determines that the supplement represents a significant risk to the public. This lack of regulation places a greater burden on the public to be knowledgeable about the supplemental products they buy.[18] Therefore, the DSHEA established three criteria for the sale of dietary supplements in retail outlets: (1) information must be displayed separately from the products; (2) information must not be false or misleading; and (3) information cannot promote a specific brand.

12. How is the freedom to choose alternative therapies protected by law?

Congressional support for alternative medicine is growing. In 1991, the Senate, under the leadership of Senator Tom Harkin (D-Iowa), directed the National Institutes of Health (NIH) to establish the Office of Alternative Medicine (OAM). Its purpose is to facilitate and conduct research on the effectiveness of alternative therapies, and then make that information available to the public. However, all has not been smooth sailing at the OAM. Its first director, Joseph Jacobs, resigned claiming that politicians and alternative medicine promoters were unwilling to wait for the results of high-quality research on therapies. They pushed for a faster, less objective system which concerned Jacobs: "As a taxpayer, I wouldn't trust what comes out of my office under a system like that."[19] Part of the problem stems from the different research concerns of alternative medicine proponents and those of the NIH. Jacobs believes that alternative therapies would get a more sympathetic, though inadequate, review "in an agency whose heart is in the clinic, not the research lab."[20]

Naturally, conventional medicine seeks to minimize competition from alternative therapies which it considers to be unscientific. The acceptance and legitimation of some alternative therapies over the years has helped to lessen this competitive spirit. Nevertheless, turf wars between alternative and conventional medicine have been waged and still exist. In a legal battle lasting fifteen years, the American Medical Association (AMA) was found guilty of "attempting to eliminate the chiropractic profession."[21] Today, chiropractors enjoy privileges at many hospitals, and insurance often covers chiropractic care. However, even within the chiropractic profession itself, serious disagreements continue over what constitutes good chiropractic care (see question 20).

Many Americans, private citizens and legislators alike, are campaigning for greater freedom of choice in health care. At least five states have passed laws protecting the right of patients to choose unconventional therapies and protecting their alternative-therapy providers from prosecution for "practicing medicine without a license." Insurers may soon also be required to cover alternative forms of licensed health care, such as acupuncture and massage therapy.

The most far-reaching legislation to protect nonharmful alternative therapies is the Access to Medical Treatment Act (H.R. 746). This bill, not yet passed as of this writing, would allow patients to be treated by all health-care practitioners who are legally authorized to provide professional health services in their state. Measures are included that would ensure that patients are fully informed, that non-FDA-approved products or devices could not be advertised, and that the products pose no more serious side effects than do conventional approaches. This requires that the safety of alternative therapies be clearly established, and that alternative providers be regulated and licensed. These requirements are highly controversial. The bill allows individuals access to a full range of options and could significantly lower health care costs. As with many other efforts to expand access to health care, the bill enjoys bipartisan support.

While many Christians may be concerned about access to a full range of health-care options, others may be alarmed about forced participation in "therapeutic" training. Companies have mandated employee participation in seminars based on New Age techniques such as teachings by mystics and faith healers, meditation, guided visualization, self-hypnosis, therapeutic touch, biofeedback, yoga, walking on fire, and inducing altered state of consciousness. The stated rationale has been to improve employee motivation, cooperation, and productivity. However, the means of achieving that goal may be an impermissible interference with the employee's sincerely held religious beliefs. Federal guidelines make it clear that, under Title VII, a company must accommodate its employee's religious beliefs. A company may not require employees to participate in such seminars if an employee's objection is based on sincerely held religious beliefs.[22]

Freedom to choose between conventional and alternative therapies requires having accurate information about their comparative effectiveness. Therefore, you should be aware of the unfounded claim that, "other than emergency medicine, 80 percent of what conventional medicine did had never been proven to be effective."[23] This is one of the "urban legends" of the alternative medicine world that is based on a 1978 Office of Technology report citing a 1960–1961 British survey of 19 physicians.[24] It was recently revealed that the source of this statistic was nothing more than an off-the-cuff remark made by Kerr L. White, one of the members of the OTA panel.[25] White made the statement as a challenge to others to find better evidence about how physicians were making decisions. Yet, White's remark is often misused in many articles to promote alternative medicine. Even if the percentage stated by White was accurate in 1960, recent studies have found that it is no longer accurate. A study in 1995 found that 82 percent of the decisions made by physicians could be backed up by research.[26]

POPULAR ALTERNATIVE THERAPIES

13. What is holistic health?

Holistic health is a complex and controversial subject. In many ways the term has become synonymous with New Age healing (see question 33). Most simply, it is the idea that true health depends on a proper balance of body, mind, and spirit. It focuses more on promoting health and wellness in persons than on curing diseases. Proponents emphasize the body's innate ability to heal itself, rather than the need for external medical interventions.

Holistic health is, in some ways, compatible with the biblical view of health. It is certainly closer than the idea that health depends only on the physical body. The biblical view of human creation teaches that people are spiritual, emotional, and relational beings who are also embodied (1 Thess. 5:23; Heb. 4:12). People's physical, emotional, relational, and spiritual dimensions are intricately interwoven to make them who they are. For this reason, any form of medicine that neglects patients' emotions, lifestyle, or relationships (both with others and with God) will fail to care for the whole person. Good health involves one's mind and one's spirit: "A joyful heart is good medicine, but a broken spirit dries up the bones" (Prov. 17:22; cf. 2 Sam. 13:2 and Prov. 3:8).

An important difference between New Age holistic health and Christianity lies in the moral realm. New Age holism usually claims that spiritual health comes from enlightenment (i.e., special understanding) and the realization that we are all gods. In that way, guilt is an illusion from which we must release ourselves. However, Christianity holds that guilt is an important aspect of health. Guilt helps the believer maintain a moral conscience and avoid unhealthy practices. Freedom from guilt only comes from admitting wrong thoughts and actions and then requesting and accepting the forgiveness that is available from God because the death of Jesus Christ has paid the penalty for our sin. New Age holistic health appears to dismiss the concept of guilt while Christianity resolves it.

In a New Age context, holism includes the unity of all people with one another and with the universe. All living beings are said to be united by a universal, impersonal, spiritual energy, known in Eastern religions as prana, chi, or Ki. In the West, it has also been called orgone, innate energy, or bioenergy. While sometimes likened to electricity or magnetism, it is totally different. Being nonphysical, it cannot be detected by instruments. Proponents admit there is no scientific evidence that it even exists. Despite this, it is foundational to many alternative therapies that claim to promote health by balancing its flow through people's bodies.

The methods used to tap into this energy are the same as those used by occultists to enter the demonic realm. Opening oneself to these forces is playing spiritual Russian roulette with a loaded gun. Christians should not involve themselves in any therapy said to manipulate life energy (see question 36).

14. What is mind–body medicine?

Mind–body medicine explores the influence of people's thoughts and emotions on the health of their bodies. Most ancient healing systems operated by this mechanism. As modern science revealed the causes of many illnesses to be physical in nature (bacteria, viruses, genes, and so forth), the role of the mind was minimized. Even gastric ulcers, once firmly believed to be caused by stress alone, are now known to be linked to certain bacteria and therefore to be treatable with antibiotics. Only if a physical cause cannot be found for an illness are the mind or emotions typically believed to play a role in these so-called psychosomatic illnesses.

However, this is not the only contemporary illustration of the mind–body connection. The placebo effect remains an enduring evidence of the importance of mind–body interactions (see question 6). Moreover, increased stress contributes significantly to the development of some illnesses, especially heart disease, although not to others, such as cancer. The body's immune and hormonal systems are also affected by stress.

Numerous ways to alleviate stress by eliciting the "relaxation response" have been examined by Herbert Benson at Harvard Medical School. Some of the most popular mind–body therapies are biofeedback, hypnosis, meditation, visualization, yoga, and breathing exercises (see questions 23, 30, 31). The common belief is that the body will benefit from training or manipulating the mind in various ways. Health insurance companies are actively promoting mind–body therapies as cost-effective, safe ways to reduce stress. While many of these bring relaxation, the degree to which they actually improve health or prevent illness is just beginning to be explored.

Claims about mind–body medicine often confuse causation and correlation. For example, many patients with a certain disease might be found to have a very high stress level. Stress and this disease are correlated, but this does not necessarily imply that stress caused the disease. Relieving stress might help the patient, yet it may not change the course of the physical disease. A serious danger here is that patients receiving the benefit of stress reduction might conclude that their disease is also being cured and therefore be less inclined to pursue treatments for the physical disease.

Mind–body therapies emphasize the role of personal responsibility in health, sometimes to the point of blaming patients for their illnesses. If the mind is crucial to curing disease, many conclude that the mind similarly caused the disease. The developer of the Simonton method of visualization (see question 30) notes: "If we are going to believe that we have the power in our own bodies to overcome cancer, then we have to admit that we also had the power to bring on the disease in the first place."[27] This outlook can lead to significant and unnecessary guilt feelings that have no basis in reality.

Mind–body therapies may alleviate some of life's stress and bring relief during illness. They may even help prevent the onset of an illness. However, their potentially comforting and preventive roles do not necessarily entail a curative role. Therefore, by all means, pursue appropriate ways to reduce the inevitable stress of daily life—always avoiding any influence from occult or other anti-Christian philosophies and practices. However, when an illness develops, be careful not to use mind–body therapies in place of more effective conventional therapies.

15. Why is cleansing a common principle in a number of alternative therapies?

A number of alternative therapies incorporate ways to cleanse the body of various toxins (i.e., poisons). With some therapies, cleansing may simply involve relocating to places with fresher air and cleaner water. Diet therapies based on natural, home-grown foods raise concerns about modern agriculture and packaging. Proponents claim that commercial foods contain pesticides, herbicides, and other chemicals that cause disease and that a return to a more natural diet will improve health.

Such so-called natural therapies are based on generally sound principles, though they should not be taken to extremes. Many people's diets in developed countries are unbalanced, and they would do well to include more fruits and vegetables. But these dietary changes alone would probably have limited effects on health. Many cultures that live "closer to nature" have shorter life expectancies than generally found in developed countries. Their "more natural" lifestyle does not protect them from the diseases that continue to ravage these countries.

Some alternative therapies promote other forms of cleansing that reportedly remove disease-causing toxins. The toxins are viewed as chemical products from the diet, stored chemicals produced in response to stress or negative energy in a person's energy field or aura. For example, traditional Ayurveda (see question 18) holds that negative thoughts, foods, and habits lead to the accumulation of *ama*. This must be flushed from the body using bloodletting, vomiting, laxatives, sinus cleansing, or enemas.[28] Deepak Chopra's modern interpretation of Ayurveda has replaced the first two methods with sesame oil massage, originally only "for the pleasure of kings," but viewed as more appealing to modern Western customers.

Cleansing in therapies based on life energy is a way to remove negative energy. This negative energy accumulates during illness and must be eliminated. Therapeutic-touch practitioners (see question 29) warn that it can be transferred from ill patients, causing harmful effects in practitioners.[29] This form of cleansing developed from the belief that demons cause disease. Few alternative therapies still associate cleansing with demons, shamanic medicine being an exception. Practicing cleansing techniques carries the same concerns as any involvement with life energy (see questions 33 and 36).

A better diet can lead to a better overall sense of well-being, whether through providing necessary nutrients or limiting unnecessary food additives. Use of purgatives, laxatives, and enemas can be medically indicated. However, their use as cleansing agents, just like their use as dietary aids, can lead to physical and psychological health problems, especially when people are already ill or depressed.

16. What is acupuncture?

Acupuncture is an alternative therapy that is growing in popularity and acceptability. It is sought mostly for the relief of pain, nausea, and vomiting. The technique is part of traditional Chinese medicine and is based on the belief that disease occurs when there are imbalances in chi or Qi (life energy). This concept was developed from the ancient idea that illness is caused by demons, whose devilish intent is present in the wind that resides in caves or tunnels. Although chi was later viewed as a natural phenomenon, the Chinese term for caves *(hsueh)* is still used by acupuncturists to designate the holes in the skin through which chi flows in and out of the body.

Various therapies claim to restore chi's balance. In acupuncture, this is usually done using fine needles to stimulate various points located over the body. The needles are inserted into the skin far enough that they won't fall out—a procedure that is usually painless. They are then twirled and may be left in for short periods. The needles are inserted into the chi holes, known today as acupoints, which are connected by "meridians." Ancient literature associated meridians with blood vessels, but modern literature views these as energy pathways. No consensus exists over the number or location of these meridians and acupoints nor is there any scientific evidence for their existence.

A National Institutes of Health (NIH) review found few high-quality research studies on acupuncture.[30] Many controlled studies found it to be no more effective in restoring health than a placebo. However, the panel concluded there was evidence that acupuncture reduced nausea and vomiting after chemotherapy or surgery and was effective at relieving dental pain. Many other claims are as yet without research support. Different explanations for the effectiveness of acupuncture have also been proposed. Acupuncture causes numerous biological changes, with the release of endorphins being the most significant. These compounds are part of the body's natural way to relieve pain. Also, pain in one area of the body can be reduced when another area is irritated, which may partially explain why the needles work. However, others believe acupuncture is nothing more than a placebo.

Acupuncture should not be used in the hope of curing an illness and should never replace effective therapies. Its low cost, relative safety, and limited effectiveness can make it a viable option for some conditions, such as pain relief in the situations specified by the NIH panel; however, caution should be exercised in choosing a practitioner. Those who adhere to its roots in traditional Chinese medicine and religion may call on spiritual powers to assist in treatments, thus exposing people to occult influences (1 Tim. 4:1; 2 Tim. 3:13–15; 4:3–4).

17. What is applied kinesiology?

Applied kinesiology is a system of diagnosis and treatment based primarily on people's muscles. George Goodheart, a chiropractor, developed kinesiology in 1964 using standard methods of testing muscle strength. Applied kinesiology focuses on the connection of muscle groups with the body's vital organs and systems. Testing the strength of these muscle groups reveals the health of these systems. Weaknesses in the muscles are said to be caused by life-energy imbalances, physical problems, dietary deficiencies, or allergies.

The most unique feature of applied kinesiology is its method of muscle testing. For example, patients hold their arms out straight. Practitioners place their fingers on the patient's arm and apply firm but gentle pressure. If the patient can resist this pressure and it feels normal to the practitioner, the systems related to that muscle are normal. If the patient cannot resist the practitioner's pressure, a problem exists. Tests on other muscles help pinpoint the problem and practitioners then gently massage "pressure points" located on the scalp or body. Most pressure points are located far from the affected muscles. The massage is believed to improve blood, lymph, and life-energy flow to the related muscles. Applied kinesiology's life-energy connections are the same as acupuncture's meridians.

Tests for allergies are very similar. Once an arm muscle is tested as above, some food to which the patient is suspected to be allergic is placed on the patient's lips or tongue. The arm muscle is retested, and if the patient resists the same pressure, no allergy exists. If the arm is weaker while the food is being held or is in contact with the mouth, the patient is allergic to it. Deficiencies in nutrients, vitamins, or minerals are also said to be similarly detectable through muscle testing.

A significant problem with applied kinesiology is that test outcomes vary depending on whether the patient or practitioner pushes first, the amount of pressure exerted, and the angle at which pressure is exerted. An instrument to standardize testing would be desirable but has yet to be developed. A popularized version of applied kinesiology called Touch for Health has led to further variants of the practice and is significantly influenced by New Age philosophy (see question 33).

There is no evidence that applied kinesiology works, either for diagnosing or treating health problems. While it may cause very little harm itself, someone could postpone a more conventional and reliable diagnosis while pursuing this method. Christians should also be cautious about the beliefs accompanying this practice. Practitioners who are strong advocates of the life-energy dimension of applied kinesiology may try to draw people more fully into the New Age worldview.

18. What is Ayurvedic medicine?

Ayurveda is the traditional medicine of India. The word literally means "science of life," and involves medical, philosophical, and religious aspects. It stresses *balance* between physical, mental, spiritual, and environmental elements. The best-known proponent of Ayurvedic medicine in the United States is Deepak Chopra, though some claim he misrepresents traditional Ayurveda. His numerous books include the best-sellers, *Quantum Healing, Perfect Health,* and *Ageless Body, Timeless Mind.* Chopra practiced modern Western medicine until becoming disillusioned with its limitations. He returned to India to learn Ayurveda from Maharishi Mahesh Yogi, who introduced the West to transcendental meditation. Maharishi bestowed Chopra with the title, "Dhanvantari (Lord of Immortality), the keeper of perfect health for the world," but revoked it after the two went their separate ways in 1993.[31]

In its traditional form, Ayurveda teaches that life is sustained by a form of nonphysical energy known as prana. This energy flows through everyone and everything, animating and sustaining the universe. True health results from a balanced flow of prana throughout the body. Imbalances lead to physical symptoms recognized as illness, aging, and death. Personality typing is also important for proper health and treatment of disorders. Each person has a combination of three basic personality types, called doshas, but one predominates. The doshas are important in maintaining balance among the organs of the body since imbalances also lead to sickness and disease.

A number of practices balance prana and doshas. Meditation is very important to reduce stress, bring about relaxation, and usher the person into an altered state of consciousness to attain insight into his or her health and spirituality. Ayurvedic practitioners use numerous products and practices to improve people's health. These include *rasayanas* (herbal supplements), gemstones, *panchakarmas* (purification procedures), diagnosis of disease by pulse monitoring, personality typing, and *yagyas* (religious ceremonies to solicit the aid of Hindu deities).[32] Removal of poisonous toxins from the body is also important using methods such as blood letting, vomiting, and bowel purging.

Many Ayurvedic preparations have been subjected to research, but there is no evidence to support the claim that these can cure disease, especially serious illness. In fact, many Ayurvedic practitioners today in India use modern pharmaceutical preparations. The lifestyle changes they recommend may be of benefit if decisions are based on sound dietary, stress-reduction, and relational principles. Ayurvedic medicine's intimate association with the transcendental-meditation movement in the United States should lead to the same cautions raised regarding meditation (see question 23). Because many Hindu and New Age beliefs underlie the principles of Ayurvedic medicine, Christians should approach it with caution and a critical mind (see question 33). Since Christians can obtain the benefits mentioned above without Ayurvedic practices, it is wise to pursue a more proven type of care.

19. What is chelation therapy?

Chelation therapy uses an FDA-approved drug, Ethylene Diamine Tetraacetic Acid (EDTA) for purposes for which it has not been approved. EDTA has long been approved to treat poisonings by heavy metals (e.g., lead or mercury). The term *chelation* comes from the Greek word for "claw." The EDTA drug molecule has a clawlike shape that helps it bind substances. When injected into the blood, it traps certain minerals such as iron, calcium, or lead. EDTA is removed from the body by the kidneys along with any trapped material. The procedure is dangerous because EDTA can cause kidney damage while it is being removed, but this risk is outweighed by the dangers of heavy-metal poisoning.

As an alternative therapy, EDTA is used primarily to treat coronary heart disease. Plaque builds up in arteries, causing blockages that reduce blood flow and, therefore, can lead to angina, tissue death, and increased blood pressure. Chelation therapy is said to remove some of the materials in plaque and thereby serves as an alternative to coronary bypass surgery and angioplasty. Proponents claim chelation therapy removes calcium from plaque and relieves other illnesses by removing toxic metals and neutralizing "free radicals" (fragments of molecules that easily cause unwanted reactions in the body). However, these claims are only supported by individual case reports, not by scientific studies. One month of chelation therapy could remove at most 0.2–0.3 percent of the calcium in plaque, given the amount of EDTA used.[33]

Furthermore, calcium makes up only a small fraction of arterial plaque, with cholesterol and fibrous tissue being much more abundant. Also, any calcium removed would quickly be replaced by calcium released from bones. Any impact of chelation therapy on free radicals would similarly not be enough to significantly reduce concentrations of these molecular fragments.

Chelation therapy should only be used in accordance with FDA approval, i.e., to remove heavy-metal poisons. The American Heart Association and physician organizations have reported many negative effects from the therapy. In alternative therapy, the risk has been reduced by administering less EDTA. However, intravenous infusions take three to four hours, usually requiring forty or more treatments over a couple of months. The complete course of therapy can cost from $3,000 to $4,000. The costs and risks are not warranted in light of the lack of evidence for the therapy's effectiveness with conditions other than heavy-metal poisoning.

20. What is chiropractic?

Chiropractic was started in the 1890s by D. D. Palmer, a grocery-store owner and healer. Chiropractic focuses on the spine and problems arising from misalignments within it that interfere with nerve function. This therapy views the nervous system as having paramount importance in the normal functioning of the whole body. Irregularities in the spine will interfere with the body's natural ability to heal itself and thus need to be corrected by spinal manipulation.

From its beginning, however, chiropractors have been divided over which problems they can relieve and what causes the relief. Palmer maintained that manipulations of the spine correct what he called "subluxations." These are viewed as physical blockages that interfere with normal nerve transmission; however, the nature, location, and very existence of subluxations has been disputed, even by chiropractors.

B. J. Palmer, son of the founder, went on to claim that subluxations are the cause of all disease. This led to a split with other chiropractors who sought a more scientific basis for chiropractic. These different approaches remain in chiropractic today. Some groups claim chiropractic can cure almost any disease and, therefore, seek to practice as the equivalent of primary-care physicians. Others use chiropractic procedures in a more limited role to resolve only specific conditions for which rigorous studies have revealed clear benefits. Most fall in between, particularly when their scope of practice includes diagnosis of common ailments. Many chiropractors also function in the capacity of naturopaths, i.e., practitioners who oppose the use of medicinal drugs and the consumption of any unnatural foods (see question 24).

What is rarely disputed is that spinal manipulations do relieve problems associated with many forms of lower-back pain. Results are often better and safer than those achieved by the use of painkillers or surgery. Chiropractors typically use X-rays and their hands to determine where manipulation is needed. The manipulation is done quickly using thrusts of the hands but with minimal force. The readjustments often produce a cracking noise. Relief may be immediate, may require a number of visits, or may come after an initial period of increased discomfort.

Chiropractors differ in their scientific foundations and their spiritual beliefs. Some chiropractors are open advocates of other New Age and shamanistic approaches to health and healing (see questions 27 and

33). Some incorporate many other alternative therapies into their practices. New Age and other beliefs and practices can be separated from the helpful manipulative techniques of chiropractic as the Christian Chiropractic Association seeks to do. Chiropractic can be a legitimate intervention bringing welcome relief for specific muscular and skeletal conditions. When consulting chiropractors, consideration should be given to any other practices and beliefs they may be promoting.

21. What are herbal remedies?

Herbal remedies are a variety of plant products sold for their health benefits. About fourteen hundred different plants are used in these products, few of which have been tested scientifically. Because they are natural, herbal remedies are said to be less harmful than pharmaceutical drugs. They are also less expensive because they have not been through as much processing or testing. To determine which herbal remedies are safe and effective, consult Varro Tyler's book, *The Honest Herbal: A Sensible Guide for the Use of Herbs and Related Remedies,* 3d ed. (New York: Pharmaceutical Products Press, 1993).

Many pharmaceutical drugs were developed from natural products by a field of science called pharmacognosy or phytochemistry. For example, aspirin is a slightly modified version of a compound found in willow bark. Penicillin is still produced from a fungus. Pharmaceutical companies regularly take herbal remedies, isolate the chemical causing the desired effect, test the drug for safety and efficacy, and then market the drug in a purified form. The pure drug may be extracted from its original source (as with penicillin) or may be manufactured synthetically (as aspirin usually is). In contrast, herbal remedies are marketed as the original plant material without any purification. They usually contain less of the active ingredients than drug formulations.

Because of federal legislation passed in 1994, herbal remedies are no longer reviewed by the Food and Drug Administration (FDA) for safety and effectiveness (see question 11). They are regulated as dietary supplements, though they are often used as drugs. This lack of regulation has created a number of problems. There is no assurance that the herbal remedy works, or even that it contains what is printed on the label. Other substances have been found in herbal remedies, occasionally including active pharmaceuticals to give them an effect. Even if the same quantity of plant material is present in different batches, the amount of any active ingredient can vary widely. Plants go though cycles in the production of medicinal products, and concentrations of active ingredients vary depending on how the plant is stored. Without standardized testing, batches of herbal remedies vary widely in their effectiveness.

While herbal remedies claim to be less harmful than pharmaceutical drugs, many are toxic. Every year people are harmed from overdoses sometimes caused by variations in potency. Herbal remedies, like all drugs, can interact with other medications, which may lead to dangerous side effects. While promoters of alternative therapies criticize the commercialism of conventional medicine, herbal remedies are also big business. Estimated sales were over $2 billion in the United States in 1995.[34] Potentially large profits are a strong incentive to promote sales and prevent regulation.

Some herbal remedies are believed to work because they have been "spiritually vitalized" (for example, Bach Flower remedies). Herbs, particularly hallucinogenic ones, are frequently used in witchcraft and shamanism to access the spirit world (see question 27). In these contexts, herbal remedies are tools to promote occult activities. Accordingly, discernment is needed, and the backgrounds of those manufacturing and promoting the preparations should be investigated.

Overall, herbal remedies with proven effectiveness can be helpful. But many others produce unknown effects, no effects, or harmful effects. Accurate information on herbal remedies can be difficult to find, but you should obtain it before using them.

22. What is homeopathy?

Homeopathic remedies use extremely diluted solutions of plant, mineral, animal, or chemical products in water or alcohol. Interest in homeopathy is strong in Europe, especially in Britain where the royal family employs the services of a homeopath. Increased popularity of homeopathy in the United States can be seen in product sales, which have risen 25 percent annually since the late 1980s, and now exceed $165 million a year.[35] Most sales are directly to consumers by mail or from health-food stores rather than through homeopathic practitioners. Preparations are not regulated in any way by the FDA because of an exemption granted in a 1938 law. In response to this popularity, some insurance companies provide coverage for homeopathy.

Modern homeopathy was founded by the German physician, Samuel Hahnemann (1755–1843). Dissatisfied with contemporary medical practices, such as bloodletting, blistering, and purging, he developed his own medical system. In experiments called "provings," he tested many different substances on himself and his assistants. The symptoms caused by the substances were meticulously recorded, and this information is still consulted today.

Hahnemann proposed the Law of Similars after observing the symptoms produced by many substances. According to this law, if a substance produces symptoms in a healthy person, it will cure people who are ill with those same symptoms. In other words, homeopaths believe that "diseases can be cured by administering minute doses of drugs which in larger amounts cause the symptoms of the particular disease being treated."[36] For example, healthy people given an extract of belladonna develop fevers, flushing, and other flu-like symptoms. The Law of Similars suggests that this diluted extract be used to treat fever or flu. Homeopaths extensively interview a patient to determine the preparation that most closely matches the patient's combination of symptoms.

The preparation chosen is diluted repeatedly with vigorous shaking at each step. Homeopaths believe dilution increases potency, in direct opposition to the common observation that more substance causes more effect. This is the most scientifically problematic aspect of homeopathy. Homeopaths admit that many extracts are so diluted that virtually none of the original extract could possibly remain.

Clinical studies have not consistently found that homeopathic preparations are any better than placebos. A few studies have noted significant improvements in health, but these studies have been criticized for not adequately ensuring that other factors were not causing the improvements. Some homeopaths believe that extracts imprint a memory on the water molecules through some electromagnetic force. No evidence of this exists. If such imprinting did occur, one would expect water to carry the memory of every substance it ever dissolved—leading to many more effects than are observed.

Hahnemann's explanation of a homeopathic effect was that the shaking involved in dilution releases "the spiritual vital force" of the healing substance. Thus, more shaking releases more energy and gives stronger effects. According to Dana Ullman, president of the Foundation for Homeopathic Education and Research, this energy is similar to prana, "the inherent, underlying, interconnective, self-healing process of the organism."[37] Thus, some proponents of homeopathy introduce patients to vitalism and life-energy ideas (see question 36).

Others claim that the extremely diluted homeopathic solutions work because people believe they work or because patients have positive interactions with practitioners. In this way, homeopathic remedies might help patients, or at least not harm them. However, patients must be careful not to neglect diagnosis and treatment of conditions that conventional medicine can cure or alleviate.

23. What is meditation?

Meditation can mean a variety of things, depending on the context. The most common forms of meditation associated with alternative therapies have their origins in Eastern religions and occult practices. Their goal is to quiet or empty the rational mind so that a person can become more aware of his or her inner self. This usually involves some state of altered consciousness that allegedly leads to true spiritual enlightenment.

In practice, the meditator relaxes in a peaceful environment. Mental attention is focused on some object, action, or thought, such as a mantra (a sacred word or formula repeated over and over again) or one's own breathing. The goal is to remain alert, but relaxed. It is this state of relaxation that is said to bring health benefits. Research shows that many illnesses are caused or exacerbated by stress. People are understandably searching for ways to relax. Since long-term meditators are able to control many body functions, meditation is seen as a way to increase control over one's body and thereby to relax it. Clinical studies on meditation have confirmed a number of health benefits, such as reduction in stress, control of chronic pain, and reduced blood pressure.

However, meditation has also been documented to cause problems. Transcendental meditation (TM), promoted by the Maharishi Mahesh Yogi, was very popular in the 1960s and did much to familiarize Americans with meditation and Hinduism. One study found that 48 percent of TM practitioners reported adverse effects, the most common being anxiety, depression, confusion, frustration, mental and physical tension, and inexplicable outbursts of antisocial behavior.[38] These were reported by TM trainers who continued with the method, not those who stopped meditating. Other studies have documented adverse effects as serious as attempted suicide and psychiatric hospitalization.[39]

The ultimate goal of most forms of meditation used with alternative therapies is spiritual insight and information related to healing. Great emphasis is placed on intuition and the insight attained during meditation and altered states of consciousness. Practitioners often encourage patients to *trust their own intuition* rather than the rational ideas of others. This unwise counsel reflects the contemporary trend to view the content of spirituality as a matter of personal preference.

The Bible counsels otherwise. At many points, it teaches that following our own intuition often leads to falsehood and deception. God repeatedly reproves people for their beliefs that they know what is best for themselves and their world (Num. 15:39; Deut. 12:8; Judg. 17:6). Insight received during altered states of consciousness is especially problematic. The false prophets of the Old Testament relied on divination and visions, revealing only the futility and deception of their own minds (Jer. 14:14; 23:16–17, 25–32; Ezek. 13:6–8). In contrast, God calls on us to do what is right *in His sight* (Exod. 15:26). His purposes and direction are revealed by the Holy Spirit's working through a variety of vehicles, including the wise counsel of mature Christians. While God may give insight and direction in various ways, communications from God are always in harmony with His written Word (1 Cor. 14:29–33; Gal. 1:8; 1 John 4:1–2). In other words, the Bible provides a basis by which to judge if a communication that apparently is from God truly is so.

Christians should retain control over their minds and thoughts at all times (2 Cor. 10:5). Altered states open people to spiritual suggestion, making them vulnerable to demonic or other unwholesome influences. Meditation is mentioned often in the Bible (Josh. 1:7–9; Ps. 1:2–3; 19:14; 49:3; 104:34; 119:97, 99). Biblical meditation challenges people to reflect daily on God's Word in a thoughtful and life-changing way. It expects them to conform to God's purpose and guidance. Contrary to TM and other forms of meditation, Christian meditation is not emptying one's mind or focusing on one's inner self; rather, it is filling one's mind with truth while focusing on the God of all truth.

24. What is naturopathy?

Naturopathy is practiced by a naturopathic doctor (ND) who uses only so-called natural means of preventing and curing illness. So-called unnatural pharmaceutical drugs and surgeries are avoided. Naturopathy is based on the same medical science as conventional medicine and uses many of the same diagnostic tools. However, differences occur in the treatments most commonly used. NDs recommend practices like homeopathy, herbal remedies, acupuncture, biofeedback, counseling, diet, and physical manipulations (see questions 16, 21, 22). NDs view a treatment's long tradition of use as significant evidence of its effectiveness.

Schools of naturopathic medicine were popular in the United States in the early 1900s, declined in popularity during the middle of the century, and have experienced renewed interest recently. The curricula for these schools' first two years is similar to that of medical schools. The second two years focus on treatments used by NDs, which are significantly different from those taught in medical schools. As of this writing, most states do not license or regulate NDs, and two states (South Carolina and Tennessee) explicitly forbid them to practice. However, in twelve states (Alaska, Arizona, Connecticut, Florida, Hawaii, New Hampshire, Maine, Montana, Oregon, Utah, Vermont, and Washington) and the District of Columbia, the ND is licensed to practice all therapies associated with naturopathy upon passing certification examinations at the end of four years of naturopathic schooling.[40] A medical doctor (MD), however, must complete an additional three years of residency to practice general medicine and must undergo even further training to practice in a specialty, such as oncology or pediatrics.

Naturopaths claim that they can treat most illnesses

and that they refer patients requiring complicated surgeries or high-tech treatments to MDs. They emphasize the importance of preventive medicine and healthy lifestyles, and they seek to use and develop the body's natural healing potential. Some health-insurance plans are covering naturopathic services because of their lower costs and fewer side effects as compared with conventional medicine.

Naturopathy emphasizes a holistic approach to health care that is sometimes compatible with a biblical approach but that can include New Age spirituality and vitalism (see question 33). Some naturopaths also claim that many illnesses arise from the accumulation of toxins in the body. These NDs recommend cleansing, sometimes through diet or exercise but also with purgative methods, some of which are very severe (see question 15). Also, consumers should be aware that while some NDs work cooperatively with MDs, others are more antagonistic. This antagonism, and their less-extensive training, could lead to delays in getting effective treatment for more serious conditions. Since some of the treatments have not demonstrated clinical effectiveness, they should not replace therapies with established effectiveness.

25. What is osteopathy?

Osteopathy is a good example of the difficulties associated with classifying therapies as alternative or conventional. Today, a doctor of osteopathy (DO) is almost indistinguishable from a medical doctor (MD). A doctor of osteopathy and a medical doctor receive very similar training at very similar schools and hospitals. But such was not always th~~case. Andrew Taylor Still started osteopathy in 1874 after becoming disillusioned with conventional medicine when his children died of meningitis. He came to believe that all diseases originate in bone misalignments; thus the therapy's name: *osteo* (meaning bone) and *pathy* (meaning disease).

Early in the twentieth century, conflict raged between doctors of osteopathy and medical doctors, with osteopathy viewed as unconventional. However, its acceptance into conventional medicine grew so that by the 1960s, doctors of osteopathy in the United States came to be accepted as equivalent to medical doctors. A key milestone in this acceptance occurred in 1958 when the American Osteopathic Association rejected some of Andrew Still's more eccentric beliefs and accepted scientific principles as the foundation for osteopathy. Today, the distinguishing characteristics of osteopathy are barely visible, to the lament of some osteopathic doctors. Some retain a more holistic approach to health care than does the typical medical doctor and incorporate some manual manipulation into their practices. Osteopathy in other countries, such as Britain and Australia, is not so widely accepted and is still viewed as a complementary therapy.

The underlying principle in osteopathy is that many illnesses arise when the body's physical structure is out of alignment. Manual manipulation helps restore balance to the physical body and cure illness. Therapies include massage and joint manipulation similar to that of chiropractors (see question 20). Exercise regimens, posture advice, and relaxation techniques may also be suggested. Osteopathy also claims to have a more holistic approach to health care than that of conventional medicine, though even some osteopaths dispute whether this is really the case.[41]

For treatment of back pain, muscle problems, and

other pain associated with movement, osteopathy has research support. However, more controversial is a practice called craniosacral therapy. Some osteopaths and chiropractors claim that this procedure manipulates the bones of the head, spine, and pelvis to allow the free flow of cerebrospinal fluid, or, as some prefer to call it, a free flow of life energy. They believe that the bones of some children may not have returned to their optimum positions after childbirth and, therefore, need to be gently massaged into place (sometimes by nontouch therapies like therapeutic touch—see question 29). However, according to accepted anatomical science, the bones of the skull are fused by age two and cannot be moved. It is, therefore, understandable why the attempt to move the bones of an infant's skull is controversial. Note that there is no documented evidence that the therapy works or is harmful.

26. What is Reiki?

Reiki (pronounced ray-key) means universal life-force energy. It is said to be the ancient healing practice that Buddha (and Jesus) used, though all records of it are lost.[42] Mikao Usui, a Zen Buddhist monk, rediscovered Reiki in the mid-1800s during a psychic experience after three weeks of meditating, fasting, and praying on Mount Koriyama in Japan. Details about lost aspects of the practice have supposedly been revealed through channeling, the New Age term for consulting spirit guides (see question 33).

Reiki is practiced and taught in a number of different ways, but the basic methods are similar. Reiki training was, until recently, conducted in secret ceremonies that practitioners were forbidden to disclose. Reiki is now being promoted in "respectable" journals. Practitioners of Reiki advance through three levels of training. To become a first-degree Reiki practitioner, the student must go through four "attunements." During these initiation ceremonies, a Reiki master opens healing channels (or chakras) within the students that fill them with life energy, called Ki, which is the same as prana and chi (see question 36). Students feel Ki flow through them, usually resulting in hot hands. Students also psychically receive a set of special symbols that later become an indispensable part of healing rituals. Reiki masters call on the help of spirit guides during attunements.

First-degree Reiki practitioners are able to detect and move life energy. In becoming a second-degree Reiki, the practitioner learns how to use the symbols received in attunements and how to send Ki over longer distances. The practitioner learns about spirit guides and how to contact and use them in healing sessions. A second-degree Reiki can attain the third degree, or Reiki master level, only by invitation of a Reiki master. During this phase, practitioners commit their lives to Reiki, come to embody life energy, and give complete control of healing sessions to their spirit guides.

In healing sessions, practitioners place both hands, extended and palms down, on or above the person's body. When the practitioner intends to heal, the life energy flows through the hands, bringing sensations of hot, cold, tingling, color, or pain. These subside after about five minutes, and the practitioner moves to another area. A complete healing session can take an hour or more. Practitioners draw or visualize the special symbols to increase the power of the energy being directed. Second- and third-degree Reiki practitioners need not be present with their patients because they are able to send Ki over long distances.

Reiki is antithetical to biblical Christianity. Channeling is a way of communicating with spirits to obtain information not otherwise accessible. It is denounced in the Bible as sorcery, mediumship, and spiritism (Lev. 19:26, 31; 20:6; Deut. 18:9–14; Acts 19:19; Gal. 5:20; Rev. 21:8). Contacting spirit guides is dangerous spiritually, physically, and emotionally (1 Peter 5:8). Reiki practitioners seek what is called the Kundalini experience (see question 31). This pinnacle of psychic experiences is known to cause severe emotional and psychological disturbances.

27. What is shamanic medicine?

Shamanic or shamanistic medicine is a group of practices by which a shaman attempts to bring healing. Shamans are priests or religious leaders in numerous tribal cultures. Among Native Americans they are called medicine men. Shamans go through extensive, specialized training to become the one member of a tribe who can contact the spirits of ancestors, animals, or demons. To reach the spirits, the shaman enters a trance, which can be induced by fasting, hallucinogenic herbs, or rituals that involve dancing, drumming, and chanting. These spirits then guide the shaman to information needed for healing, among other things. Shamans can avert adverse events if they find ways to appease the offended spirits or demons. The shaman then returns to normal consciousness with this information.

Shamans practice occult and magical activities that are clearly forbidden in the Bible (Lev. 19:26, 31; 20:6; Acts 19:19; Gal. 5:20; Rev. 21:8). King Saul's use of a medium to contact the deceased spirit of Samuel demonstrates that people can contact spirits (1 Sam. 28). But Saul was condemned by God for using such a medium.

Instead, he should have sought guidance from the Lord (1 Chron. 10:13–14). Occult practitioners (e.g., diviners, dreamers, and soothsayers) and activities (e.g., sorcery, spells, and astrology) work to misdirect people in their greatest hours of need (Isa. 47:9–13). The source people choose to provide the answers they seek affects not only their physical welfare, but may also influence their eternal destiny (Jer. 27:9–10).

While God condemns occult practices (Deut. 18:9–14), He recognizes that we need spiritual guidance. God sent specifically chosen prophets to reveal truths about Himself and His world that we need to know. These prophets were identified by the accuracy of their message (Deut. 18:15–22). The message of these prophets and of Christ's apostles were compiled to give us the Bible so that everyone could have access to true spiritual guidance (2 Peter 1:20–21) and thereby distinguish truth from error. However, we must accept the fact that God has revealed only what we need to know (Deut. 29:29). Shamans use occult practices in attempts to discover things that we have no need to know or should not know because the knowledge may harm us.

During their training, shamans are possessed by either their spirit guides or the spirit of their "power animal" (a spirit with the form of an animal). Any healing done by the shaman is due to the spirits, which may enter or possess the person in need of healing. Possession is not only spiritually dangerous but can lead to serious mental illness and physical suffering. Shamans blame many diseases on evil spirits; therefore, healing ceremonies are often conflicts among spirits. Shamans also incorporate herbal remedies, meditation, and visualization (see questions 21, 23, 30) into their practices. People have made use of some shamanic practices without following shamanism, but these practices introduce them to the belief system and, therefore, may expose them to demonic oppression—or possession in the case of non-Christians.

28. What is shark cartilage therapy?

Shark cartilage is a treatment for cancer promoted most vigorously by Dr. William Lane, who wrote *Sharks Don't Get Cancer* in 1992; and *Sharks Still Don't Get Cancer* in 1996. Although sharks do get cancer, the therapy is generally based on scientifically plausible ideas.[43] Cartilage contains no blood vessels, while cancers require extensive blood supplies to grow. If cartilage inhibits the growth of blood vessels, it might also inhibit cancer growth. Early studies showed that cartilage from cows, and an extract from it, did slow the growth of blood vessels in laboratory animals.

These studies, and later ones that discussed the use of shark cartilage, prompted William Lane to do further studies. Sharks have no bones, so cartilage is the most abundant compound in their skeletal system. Lane extracted shark cartilage and tested the product on humans in cancer clinics in Cuba and Mexico. This testing led to three publications that are used to support shark cartilage's effectiveness against cancer. One study contained only eight patients and no control group. The second only reported differences in the microscope slides made of the tumors in treated and untreated animals. The third reported interviews with twenty-one cancer patients who contacted Lane to express their appreciation for his product. Taken together, these constitute extremely weak evidence for effectiveness.

In shark cartilage therapy, about sixty to ninety grams of cartilage must be taken daily. The extract consists mostly of proteins, which are probably destroyed during digestion. While there is no evidence that shark cartilage is harmful (other than nausea from the taste and from the large quantities), there is little or no evidence that it inhibits the spread of cancer. However, when taking the extract delays cancer patients from pursuing effective treatments, the probability of achieving a cure or remission is likely to diminish. Shark cartilage costs about $700 a month. This is a high price to pay for a therapy that shows little evidence of success, especially when potentially more effective therapies are available.

29. What is therapeutic touch?

Therapeutic touch (TT) is a therapy widely promoted in nursing, with dozens of nursing colleges teaching it and tens of thousands of nurses trained in it. It was developed in the 1970s by a nursing professor, Dolores Krieger, along with Dora Kunz, a self-proclaimed clairvoyant and then president of the Theosophical Society in America. Theosophy is a blending together of ancient philosophies, Eastern religions, and occult practices. It played an important role in developing the beliefs foundational to the New Age movement.

Practitioners claim TT is a modern version of the biblical laying on of hands. However, ancient Jewish writings never associate the laying on of hands with healing. Instead, it was a way to impart divine blessing or commissioning (e.g., Num. 27:18–19). The New Testament describes the laying on of hands in similar ways (Matt. 19:13–15; Acts 6:6; 1 Tim. 4:14) and also as part of healing (Mark 5:23). However, the healing was not attributed to the practice of putting hands on the person but to the power of God.

Placing hands on a person has been noted as a distinguishing feature of Jesus' healing ministry. It must certainly have been an amazing experience for a seriously ill person to be touched by the hand of the Messiah (Matt. 8:3). Physical touch is comforting and reassuring, especially when someone is sick or anxious. Modern health-care settings often neglect this, and practitioners of TT claim to be bringing this emphasis back into health care. However, this claim ignores the important fact that TT *does not* involve physical touch. Instead, proponents of TT believe that life energy, in the form of a person's aura, extends a few inches beyond people's skin. This is the same energy known as prana in Hindu medicine and chi in Chinese medicine (see question 36).

Although Kunz claims she sees these energy fields, Krieger and most practitioners do not. Instead, practitioners must enter a state of meditation called "centering." This altered state of consciousness allows people to quiet their minds and contact their "inner selves." In this state, TT therapists get guidance about the energy fields of the people they are trying to treat. While remaining in this state, practitioners pass their hands a few inches above patients' bodies. Although some practitioners touch patients, teachers emphasize that physical contact is not necessary.

TT therapists believe that good health requires a balanced energy field. Problems are detected through "vague hunches, passing impressions, flights of fancy, or, in precious moments, true insights or intuitions."[44] Imbalances and blockages can be cleared if the energy field is smoothed by passing the hands over the aura accompanied by the practitioner's intention to help and heal. TT is said to reduce anxiety, relieve pain, and accelerate wound healing, but many studies have found it is no better than a placebo. Studies with positive results have been shown to be poorly designed or improperly interpreted.

The beliefs and practices promoted as TT are commonly found in Eastern religions, theosophy, and New Age writings (see question 33). Krieger, a Buddhist, admits that TT is based on the same principles as Buddhism. Theosophical and occult writings have long described a practice called pranic (or auric) healing. This is identical to TT and includes the lack of physical contact, emphasis on energy fields, importance of meditation, and even the shaking of one's hands to remove "negative energy."[45]

Prominent practitioners of TT warn that the practice can cause harm, such as depression, irritability, increased physical pain, restlessness, nausea, dizziness, and disorientation, especially with very young children, the elderly, and the frail.[46] These harms have not been verified by research, but they appear reasonable due to the altered state of consciousness induced in patients. Given these warnings, the lack of evidence for its effectiveness, and the connection with occult beliefs and practices, Christians would be wise to avoid TT completely.

30. What are visualization techniques?

Visualization techniques, or imagery, are ways people use to tap into the power of the imagination and the mind to influence physical processes. Most often, people are asked to sit or lie comfortably, close their eyes, and imagine some relaxing scene or image. This could be an actual place once visited or a color one finds relaxing. Guided imagery is where someone describes a scene while others picture it in their minds. Music is often added to enhance the setting.

Visualization is said to have the same benefits as meditation and other relaxation therapies. Many of the same physiological responses occur during visualization. Visualizing food can cause the production of saliva, so visualization of cells fighting a disease is said to stimulate the immune system. The Simonton method of guided imagery was developed by an oncologist and his wife in the 1970s. In this method, patients visualize their cells fighting and consuming their cancer cells. Well-designed studies have found no evidence that visualization lessens any disease or complements other treatments, although relaxation is produced.

Alternative therapies incorporate various forms of visualization. Some are ways to find guidance from one's inner self or to contact spirit guides. Krieger's book on therapeutic touch (see question 29) uses guided imagery to contact and gain insight from a "luminous child" (a self-consciously created image who appears while in a centered or meditative state) who should be trusted and with whom one should identify.[47] At this point, visualization ceases being an innocent remembrance of pleasant experiences and becomes an occult activity.

New Age philosophy promotes visualization because of the belief that thoughts create reality (see question 33). Two proponents state: "The thoughts and images that we hold in our minds are not just abstract, ineffectual ideas or neurons firing in our brains. They actively shape reality."[48] But in going deeper into one's own psyche, there can be serious dangers, as there are with meditation (see question 23). These same authors claim: "By naively adopting certain visualization practices, we may well endanger our mental and physical health not only in this lifetime *but in future embodiments as well. . . .*

69

Even if a person does not suffer any adverse side effects now, the connection with the lower realms has been made and will take effect in the future" (emphasis in the original).

Some forms of visualization about neutral images can be helpful ways to relax. They are used sometimes in counseling sessions. Other forms are ways to contact our inner selves or the spiritual realm. If visualization is recommended, ask for a complete description of what will be involved before participating. If practiced in the context of other New Age therapies or as a way to contact spirit guides, it should be avoided completely.

31. What is yoga?

Yoga literally means "union" and is closely related to Hindu religion. It involves a variety of ways by which people achieve union of body, mind, and spirit, and also union with the ultimate reality or divine spirit. Although generally viewed in the West as a set of exercises that improve flexibility, strength, and relaxation, it is a deeply religious practice in the East. yoga basically involves breathing and posture exercises. Breathing is important not only for relaxation but also for its connection with prana, or life energy (see question 36). Improved flow of prana is at least as important in yoga as any physical benefits. As students advance in yoga, moral and character changes are expected with the ultimate goal being the realization of their divine nature.

Clinical research shows that yoga exercises can improve physical fitness, reduce stress, and help relieve chronic pain. Its benefits come only with sustained, regular practice, which may involve many hours each week. However, it does not cure illness, and the postures and physical exertion may cause physical problems. As with any exercise program, people should ensure they have no underlying health problems and start slowly.

While yoga can be simply a form of exercise, its basic purpose is spiritual. People who start yoga as a form of exercise will soon find themselves exposed to its religious teachings. Gradually, people may find themselves seeking the spiritual enlightenment that yoga was originally designed to produce. The pinnacle of such enlightenment is called Kundalini arousal. In Hindu mythology, Kundalini is the serpent goddess who rests at the base of the spine. When aroused, the serpent travels up the spine, activating a person's prana and clearing the person's chakras. Clearing the chakras activates various psychic abilities, including healing powers. Ultimately, Kundalini reaches the chakra in the head—opening practitioners to enlightenment from occult sources (cf. receiving Reiki symbols, see question 26).

Yoga is an alternative therapy which is difficult to wholeheartedly accept or reject. As a set of physical and breathing exercises, it can improve general well-being. As a deeply religious practice with the goal of union with the divine, it is antithetical to biblical Christianity. In spite of its reputation as a simple calisthenics program, reports of physical and spiritual harm continue to surface.

While there may not be clear reasons for Christians to condemn all forms of yoga, Paul gives some helpful advice: "All things are lawful for me, but not all things are profitable" (1 Cor. 6:12). Given its origin and risks, the burden rests with the yoga advocate to demonstrate why this form of exercise and relaxation should be chosen when so many other forms exist that have no spiritual underpinnings.

32. Is alternative therapies' attention to spirituality positive?

Many alternative therapies are part of the holistic health movement that emphasizes the importance of body, mind, and spirit in health care. The recognition of the role and importance of spirituality in people's lives is a significant improvement over the way it has been neglected and rejected for most of this century. With the rapid advancement of technology, science has become a philosophy of life, not just a tool for understanding the created world. For many people, anything that cannot be scientifically validated is either nonexistent or not important. Spiritual issues fall into this category, and hence their role in health and healing is dismissed.

Attempts to use the idea of human evolution to inject meaning and purpose into a purely physical life have proved hollow. People have been left searching for ways to understand and give meaning to life, death, and suffering. Into this void has come a plethora of ideas grouped under the term *spirituality*. Proponents of alternative therapies view spirituality as attention to one's inner being and a search for meaning. They criticize those who seek only material gain, either for their own bodies or through possessions. Biblically, this response to life is appropriate, given God's self-revelation to all people (Rom. 1:18–20). Christians should welcome the opportunity to dialogue with others about spiritual meaning. We can welcome the openness to discuss our faith and spiritual values, which even recently would have been dismissed as "unscientific."

However, Christians must oppose the idea that the content of one's spirituality is whatever one believes or wants it to be. In today's postmodern culture, spirituality is seen pragmatically as a means toward health, not as a search for truth about the spiritual realm (e.g., humanity's fallen nature and need for God). For so many today, it doesn't matter whether spirituality is viewed as psychological peace, harmony with nature, contact with spirit guides, or a relationship with the Creator God of the Bible. Promoters of alternative therapies generally hold that people should be open to trying anything that might lead to spiritual enlightenment. Whether altered states of consciousness or contact with spirit guides is the goal, people are encouraged to try new practices and therapies.

Christians must reject this approach to spirituality. The Bible declares that there is only one true God, and He has established only one path to spiritual health (Exod. 20:2–5; John 14:6). But there is also a spiritual reality that seeks to deceive and harm people (John 8:44; 1 Peter 5:8). The evil one lures people away from God by convincing them that all forms of spirituality are equally valid. He may even allow them to have positive experiences to entice them into further occult-based activities (2 Thess. 2:7–12). For this reason, Christians must test all forms of spirituality to determine if they are from God (1 John 4:1–3).

33. How strongly are alternative therapies linked to Eastern religions, New Age beliefs, and the occult?

Some alternative therapies have no religious connections. For example, many herbs, diets, and instruments are promoted simply as alternatives to conventional drugs and technology. However, there is also a strong undercurrent of religious ideas behind some alternative therapies. The *New Age Journal* has noted increased interest in holistic health as the most significant change contributing to the redefining of American culture, presumably redefined according to New Age beliefs.[49] Part of the attractiveness of alternative therapies is their form of spirituality.

A large group of alternative therapies are based on life energy (see question 36). The existence and properties of this energy are intertwined with Eastern mystical religions, New Age philosophy, the occult, and vitalistic belief systems. For example, Prana is the name of the supreme god of Hindu Vedic religion that claims that the world was created through this "one god above all gods" and "lord of all created things."[50]

Healing plays an important role in occult activity. "It is said in the occult books . . . that all initiates must be *healers*."[51] White witchcraft is similar: "Healing has been a central part of witches' activity from time immemorial, and it remains so today."[52] Much occult healing makes use of life energy, or prana. "Merely to increase the circulation of Prana is sufficient to cure many minor diseases."[53] Occult writings describe therapies for manipulating prana (i.e., pranic or auric healing) that are identical to therapeutic touch (see question 29).[54]

Many life-energy therapies have clear connections to the occult. One alternative medicine encyclopedia notes that life force or prana "can be harnessed by the individual who sensitizes himself by certain occult practices," including meditation, deep breathing, chanting mantras, advanced visualization and "secret rituals which have been closely guarded secrets of the highest mystery schools on earth . . . and beyond."[55] Dolores Krieger, cofounder of therapeutic touch, admits there is a high occult factor in how therapeutic touch works.[56] She recommends divination to obtain insight for the practice.[57] She has noticed that as her students learn therapeutic touch, "sensitivity to others as well as personal psychic sensitivity deepens. . . . Many who undergo these changes in awareness feel that they can also communicate with and understand other sentient beings, such as trees, birds, animals, as well as human beings."[58]

Some alternative therapies, such as Reiki and shamanic medicine (see questions 26 and 27), overtly recommend the use of spirit guides. Practitioners of some other therapies deny any religious dimension to their therapies, yet promote Eastern, New Age, and occult beliefs under the guise of health care. These practitioners become proselytizers, not genuine health-care providers. God wants people to be healthy. But He is also very concerned about how they become healthy. Contrary to New Age claims, there are two forms of spirit: good and evil. Scripture states that the spiritual forces of evil are very powerful. Christians should be careful to avoid any dealings with these occult spirits and powers (Lev. 19:26, 31; 20:6, 27; Deut. 18:9–14; Isa. 8:19; Jer. 14:14; Acts 19:18–19; Gal. 5:19–20).

34. Is alternative medicine in harmony with Christian tradition?

Christian tradition has always emphasized the importance of bringing healing to those who are ill. God declared Himself to be Israel's Healer (Exod. 15:26), and part of Jesus' ministry was to heal the sick. The early church continued this tradition of involvement in healing. Historians of medicine have concluded that the early church's impact on illness and health care was profound. This impact continued through the centuries.

The healing that Christianity supports is holistic in the broadest sense, encompassing physical, emotional, spiritual, moral, and relational healing. The compassionate care given by Christians over the centuries is a far cry from the cold, impersonal ways patients are sometimes treated in modern health-care facilities. In fact, both Christianity and modern alternative therapy respond negatively to any delivery of medicine that focuses on physical and psychological needs at the expense or exclusion of the spiritual.

However, Christian tradition is also at odds with the kind of spirituality that alternative therapies promote. The early church fathers frequently addressed illegitimate, magical means of healing that were especially popular with the cult of Asclepius, the Greek and Roman god of healing. For example, Augustine approved of taking herbs for stomach pain but disapproved of wearing them as charms for the same purpose.[59]

The early church also responded negatively to physicians who, in addition to healing, would promote anti-Christian philosophies. Early Christian leaders were noted for discouraging their disciples from visiting "philosopher-physicians." In the third century, Origen complained that physicians too often used their influence and position to teach philosophies that contradicted Christianity.[60] He had in mind teachings about reincarnation and the view that human beings and all other forms of life have the same type of spirit—ideas that are common among today's promoters of alternative therapies.

In contrast to magical or energy healing, the healing

power of God is not an inanimate supernatural force. God is a personal, compassionate Being who sympathizes with our suffering and to whom we can bring all our concerns, including physical health (James 5:14–16). When our physical health and well-being are threatened, we go to Him in prayer, dependent on Him even though He may not bring healing. While we actively pursue medications and therapies that have been graciously provided to us in this world by God, we must never subject ourselves to any spiritual force—no matter what its claim—that contradicts the guidelines given to us by God in His holy Word. In the fourth century, John Chrysostom lauds a Christian woman for refusing to recite magical incantations and put magical amulets on her sick child. Unwilling to disobey the Lord, "she chose rather to see her child dead, than to put up with idolatry."[61] She knew that to turn to magic instead of to the Lord would undermine her testimony to others about the importance of trusting God—and would perhaps have eternal consequences for her in heaven as well.

Living in this fallen world is a guarantee that each of us will die from some injury or illness. How should we live in light of such a reality? Christians must live by faith. We must trust in the Creator whose love for the world provided a complete remedy for physical and spiritual death in the person of His only Son, our Savior, Jesus Christ. Though we will all die in this world, those who trust in Him will never die again but will live eternally with God. However, even in this world, our faith in God will strengthen and sustain us.

A famous fourth-century leader of the church, Jerome, described in his *Letters* (39.2) how Christians could cope effectively with illness: "Am I in good health? I thank my Creator. Am I sick? In this also I praise God's will. For 'When I am weak, then I am strong,' and the strength of the spirit is made perfect in the weakness of the flesh." This faithful outlook was expressed when little was available to help overcome illness. May we who have been blessed with the best health care and public-health resources ever available express such an unfailing faith no matter what challenges to our health we face. We must not forsake the One who has promised never to forsake us (John 14:15–18, 27–28; Heb. 13:5).

35. Am I compromising my faith by using alternative therapies?

To answer this question, clear terminology is needed. In question 3, five categories of alternative therapies were described. Clear lines cannot be drawn between them, but they suggest helpful guidelines in answering this question. Christian faith can be enhanced by some aspects of alternative therapies, will be unaffected by others, and could easily be compromised by others.

Complementary therapies include such interventions as proper diet, exercise, prayer, and biblically defined approaches to spirituality (see question 37). Pursuit of these in an appropriately balanced way can enhance one's health. We should maintain our health as good stewards of our bodies and lives to serve others and glorify God. However, any good thing can be pursued excessively. When good health and personal comfort are consistently put ahead of others' needs, or pursued in ways antithetical to God's ways, we can be led away from the abundant life God offers.

Scientifically unproven therapies include shark cartilage, chelation therapy, and many herbal remedies (see questions 19, 21, 28). For the most part, these therapies do not raise spiritual concerns so long as their pursuit is balanced. Questions of cost and harm are most important, especially in light of the biblical emphasis on using our money wisely.

Scientifically questionable therapies include homeopathy and many of the therapies in the category of life-energy therapies (see question 22). Stewardship of resources should lead us to be very cautious in using these. If the explanations for how they work are at odds with well-established research, their use is unlikely to bring lasting help. Christians should have even greater concerns for scientifically questionable therapies that also fall into the next category.

Life-energy therapies can be broken into two subgroups. Some cannot be separated from their spiritual roots, such as therapeutic touch, Reiki, and shamanic medicine (see questions 26, 27, 29). Others, such as acupuncture, visualization, and yoga (see questions 16, 30, 31), are believed by some to use life energy, but others suggest they work only by natural mechanisms. The first group is clearly linked to contacting spiritual forces that are not from God and should always be avoided. The second group may have some value if they are completely removed from life-energy practitioners and philosophies. Therefore, in light of the grave dangers of involvement with life energy, it is wise to avoid any life-energy therapy. This category carries the greatest potential for compromising people's faith. Consumers should also be aware that some practitioners will incorporate life-energy techniques in therapies generally found in other categories.

Quackery and fraud can occur in conventional and

alternative medicine and clearly violate God's will (Ezek. 22:27–29). Quackery thrives when people accept therapies uncritically and without understanding them. As the saying goes, "the road to hell is paved by good intentions." God expects us to protect the ill and weak who are close to his heart (Jer. 22:16–17; 1 John 3:17). Allowing them to be taken advantage of by frauds, or by well-meaning promoters of ineffective therapies, is a violation of biblical justice.

36. Is chi or prana the same as the Holy Spirit by another name?

A number of alternative therapies are based on a vital energy, or life force, known as chi or Qi in Chinese traditions (pronounced chee), as prana in India, and as Ki in Japan. According to these belief systems, the basic substance of the universe, including human bodies, is not matter but energy and information. These same beliefs exist in Western occult traditions, as a book on witchcraft notes: "The right control of prana involves the recognition that energy is the sum total of existence and of manifestation."[62]

In this view, life energy is nonphysical and universal, animating and sustaining all living things. True health results from a balanced flow of this energy through the body and its unblocked exchange with the environment through channels called chakras. These are the essential means by which life energy is transformed into physical matter and energy. However, therapies differ on how many chakras exist and where they are located. Regardless, imbalances or blockages in the flow of life energy lead to the physical symptoms of illness, aging and death.

Belief in this life force pervades alternative therapies,

such as therapeutic touch, applied kinesiology, Ayurvedic medicine, Reiki, and hundreds of other therapies (see questions 17, 18, 26, 29). Some acupuncturists believe that their needles are inserted into channels through which this vital energy flows (see question 16). Chiropractic, herbal medicine, and homeopathy are believed by some to work by influencing this energy, although other practitioners describe their therapies in purely physical terms (see questions 20, 21, 22). One alternative therapist claims: "No matter what therapies a traditional healer depends upon, he or she essentially is treating the life force itself."[63]

Since this energy is nonphysical, no instruments can detect or measure it. Some claim the images produced by kirlian photography portray the energy field, but these have been shown to have purely physical origins.[64] People become more sensitive to life energy through training and meditation. Once in an altered state of consciousness, people can begin to detect this energy. Trained practitioners say they sense the energy field, or aura, around a person, though some claim to see it in various colors and shapes. The different therapies bring healing by removing imbalances or blockages in the flow of life energy.

Some Christians suggest that life energy is another name for God or the Holy Spirit. Assuming this, they claim that Christians should practice life-energy therapies while calling on the Holy Spirit to bring about healing. However, this cannot be the case. God is a personal being with thoughts, emotions, and a will. Life energy is an impersonal force that practitioners seek to manipulate and use for human well-being. We can (and should) pray to God for healing (James 5:14–16), but we cannot expect to control God's power like an energy field

(Luke 4:22–27; Acts 8:18–23). Yet this is precisely what all life-energy therapies seek to do.

The problem with the world is not the blocking of life energy; rather, it is human sin that has corrupted and is destroying creation. And the solution for the world is not *helping* God, in the form of life energy, to flow freely through the material universe. The solution comes when people individually respond to the convicting influence of the Holy Spirit through repentance. Although non-Christians can speak about an energy or force, this energy cannot be equated with the Holy Spirit. The Holy Spirit of the Bible only indwells believers (Eph. 1:13).

37. Is prayer an alternative therapy?

Prayer takes many forms and can mean many different things depending on the tradition within which it is practiced. Its efficacy in promoting health and healing has drawn widespread attention. Healing prayer's most popular proponent is Larry Dossey, author of the books, *Healing Words, Prayer is Good Medicine,* and *Be Careful What You Pray For*.

Dossey claims that the minds of all people are part of one unified consciousness. Thus, the thoughts of one person can affect the health of another in much the same way that our own minds affect our bodies. He claims that what is said in prayer is irrelevant. The most important aspect is one's attitude of prayerfulness. This is "a sense of simply being attuned or aligned with 'something higher.'" Instead of trying to determine what will happen through our prayers, the best attitude is one that accepts that "the outcome is always in the direction of 'what's best for the organism.'" That is, we need to concern ourselves with the overall good of the one unified consciousness.

Dossey rejects the biblical view of prayer as "antiquated and incomplete." Yet the one study that he cites to back up his claims about the healing benefits of prayer involved born-again Christians (actively involved in prayer and fellowship) praying to the God of the Bible for rapid recoveries and prevention of complications in patients.[65] While it would not be surprising to find positive health effects from the relaxation and stress reduction that should accompany prayer (Phil. 4:6–7)—or even from some people's praying for others (e.g., see James 5:14–16) —such will not always be the case. The odd thing about the study of prayer is the assumption that its effect on illness can be measured by empirical observation as if petitioners making the same prayer in a similar circumstance will necessarily produce the same result. The flaw here is that while clinical studies must control as many variables as possible, they cannot control God. If prayer was an energy, or a technique, it might be more amenable to comprehensive study. However, Christian prayer is offered to a personal God who has the final say in whether or how to answer the prayer. The Bible is clear that God does not promise to grant all prayer requests— only those that are according to His will (Matt. 7:11; 1 John 5:14). As difficult as it may be for us to accept, physical healing may not always be God's will for us (see question 39). A number of New Testament men who presumably prayed about their illnesses did not recover immediately: Timothy (1 Tim. 5:23), Trophimus (2 Tim. 4:20), and Epaphroditus (Phil. 2:30). Paul, too, prayed that the thorn in his flesh (thought by many to have been an illness) would be removed, yet it was not (2 Cor. 12:7–10). While prayer expresses the sincere desire of our hearts, the depth of our faith helps us to live with His answer (see question 38).

Prayer, then, is not so much an alternative therapy as it is an important part of any therapy we pursue. While we can pray for healing, and God may heal us—often through some form of health care—we also learn through prayer to be content in the midst of any circumstance (Phil. 4:11–13). God promises to remain with us and comfort us in our pain and suffering (Rom. 8:35–39). The willingness to pray shows a dependence and trust in God apart from oneself. Prayer is crying out to God in our pain and humbly accepting His will for our lives. In fact, prayer is a corporate activity for Christians through which we bring one another's concerns to God and praise Him for the blessings He provides. Prayer is also an opportunity to thank God for the strength and insight that we gain from trusting in Him while enduring hardship.

38. *What should I think about faith healing?*

Faith healing is usually associated either with persons who claim to have a divine gift of healing or with prayer to a higher power. Faith healing was an important part of both Jesus' ministry and that of the early church. For Jesus, faith generally preceded a healing (Matt. 13:58; Mark 6:5–6); however, at times He performed healing to show His authority and power over creation as the divine Son of God (Matt. 8:28–34; John 9:35–41; 11:45). Jesus commissioned His disciples to participate in His healing ministry (Matt. 10:1–5; Luke 10:9), a role that continued throughout the early years of the church (Acts 3:1–11; 5:15–16; 9:33–34; 14:8–10). The ability to perform healing and miracles is mentioned by Paul in his list of gifts (1 Cor. 12:9–10), but the practice appears to lessen as the church matures. By the time of James' writing, believers are advised to pray for healing (James 5:13–18).

Some debate occurs among Christians as to whether miraculous faith healing occurs today. All agree that God still heals people, with the gift of salvation being the most profound form of healing a person can experience. Because salvation comes through faith in the atoning work of Jesus Christ (Eph. 2:8–9) it might be called a form of faith healing, though spiritual in nature. As Christians grow in their relationship with God, they change in ways that bring spiritual, emotional, and relational health (Col. 3:9–17). These factors alone may lead to physical healing but, of course, there is no guarantee. Because such change comes as a result of faith (Gal. 3:1–5), they too may be considered a form of faith healing.

However, whether God still grants miraculous physical cures of the type found in the Bible is debated. Some groups claim that since salvation comes by faith and brings spiritual healing, physical healing also comes by faith in Jesus Christ. These people believe all physical ailments can be healed if a person has enough faith. Matthew 8:16–17 is used to argue this position, along with other passages on prayer (Matt. 7:7–8; James 5:13–18). These ideas have become part of the so-called health and wealth gospel.

However, a more complete understanding of the biblical teaching holds that God Himself can heal people miraculously, though the reasons for healing in the New Testament are rarely applicable today. In New Testament times, miracles served an important purpose in authenticating the message of those performing them. Thus, the miracles of Jesus were performed to show witnesses that Jesus' claim to be the Son of God was legitimate. They were not simply demonstrations of power. Similarly, the miracles performed by the early church legitimatized the apostles' message by associating it with the message and ministry of Jesus. Since the gospel no longer needs this type of legitimization, healing miracles are no longer necessary (except perhaps in the rare instance where the gospel reaches a community never before exposed to Christianity).

Nevertheless, God's miraculous intervention is possible. As illustrated in the ministry of Jesus, certain criteria are typically present. Jesus' miracles were complete, lasting, instantaneous, and easily verifiable, such as when well-known lame and blind men were healed (John 5:5–9; 9:8). These miracles are quite different from the so-called divine and miraculous healing performed at modern faith-healing services. Neither the ill, nor God, are served when people get caught up in the euphoria of misguided hope and incorrectly claim that a miracle has occurred. James Randi (in *The Faith Healers*) has shown that suspicion concerning the work of modern-day faith healers is warranted. Often there is no clear evidence that the condition was both present before the healing took place and absent afterward. Most of the work of modern-day faith healers can be rejected because it does not satisfy the criteria of biblical healing and fails to direct one's loyalty to God alone.

At the same time, Christians should not dismiss the idea that *God can, and may, choose to miraculously heal someone today*. Whether through prayer or through medical intervention, healing ultimately rests with trust in God. In spite of illness, disability, or bad circumstance, God's love never fails (Rom. 8:35–39). Often the presence of suffering serves as a tutor to teach us about His presence and comfort so that we will be able to comfort others (2 Cor. 1:3–7). Trust in God teaches us how to be content in all circumstances (Phil. 4:11–13). He alone is the One who will ultimately help us who love Him make sense of the ups and downs of life in a fallen world.

39. Does all healing come from God?

Some Christians claim that we should be open to alternative therapies since all healing comes from God. Nothing could be further from the truth. God wants to grant physical healing. Jesus is the Great Physician, and God alone was Israel's Healer (Exod. 15:26). But the means to those ends are very important to God. The Bible describes a number of conflicts between legitimate and illegitimate approaches to healing. King Ahaziah sought out the god Baal when he was seriously injured and was condemned for doing so (2 Kings 1:2–4). When King Asa developed a serious illness, he was condemned for depending on physicians instead of depending on God (2 Chron. 16:12).

Some commentators on Asa have concluded that the Bible advocates seeking only divine healing. However, the context is clear that Asa's primary problem was his refusal to turn to God for help. In fact, the physicians referred to here were most likely Gentiles who practiced pagan magical healing since these would have been the only groups likely to have existed in that day.[66] Numerous biblical references suggest that using effective medical therapies is completely appropriate. Some of those mentioned are cleansing, bandaging, soothing with oil (Isa. 1:5–6) or balm (Jer. 8:22; 46:11; 51:8), and setting fractures (Ezek. 30:21). Physicians are not generally viewed negatively (Jer. 8:22; Luke 5:31; Col. 4:14).

However, God will not always allow such means to

be effective. While the promise of complete healing will be fulfilled in eternity, God chooses for now not to heal some people. Good health is not an automatic indication of God's blessing, just as illness and misfortune do not automatically indicate God's judgment (Luke 13:1–5; John 9:1–3). God may decide that healing a person may not be the best thing in a specific situation. Job is the clearest example of a faithful servant of God who suffered much. Dorcas was a disciple "full of good works," but she got sick and died (Acts 9:36–37). Timothy appears to have been sickly (1 Tim. 5:23). Epaphroditus became sick while doing the work of ministry (Phil. 2:25–30). James anticipates that believers will get ill (James 5:14–16). As in Job's case, Satan may be the source of the illness. At other times he may masquerade as an angel of light in an attempt to deceive or mislead people (Matt. 24:24; 2 Cor. 11:14–15; Rev. 13:14). God may allow us to learn important lessons from the limitations imposed by illness. How many of us might never learn to appropriately depend on God and others if we did not have to grapple with illness and disability?

Whether one's good health or illness is of God or is the work of Satan, ultimately we as Christians know that God is overseeing each and every detail of our lives, molding and shaping us into the image of His son. We must place our trust in the intervention of a sovereign God, not in the uncertainties of conventional or alternative intervention. While God wants all people to have good health, the means by which good health is obtained are very important to Him. Do our decisions reflect His sovereignty and our personal trust in His will, or do they reflect fear and despair? Our relationship with God matters, for through it we gain confidence and an immovable faith that will both serve us and others until death or Christ's return. As difficult as it may sound, God is more concerned about our obedience and faithfulness to Him than He is about our physical well-being (Matt. 18:7–9).

We cannot assume that all methods for healing ultimately please God. Great signs and wonders will be accomplished by Satan and the Beast, including the healing of a fatal wound (Rev. 13). With these powers available to the evil one, we must be wary of claims that all healing comes only from God. In contrast, it may sometimes be God's will that we put ourselves at risk of illness, injury, or even death for the sake of others and our relationship with our Father (Matt. 16:24–26; Acts 5:27–32, 40–42). Our task is to trust in God and serve Him alone. "My beloved children, be steadfast, immovable, always abounding in the work of the Lord, knowing that your toil is not in vain in the Lord" (1 Cor. 15:58).

Conclusion

We have only briefly touched on some of the most popular alternative therapies available. It should be more clear now why it is ill-advised to make sweeping statements about whether alternative therapies (as an entire group) should be accepted or rejected. Instead, each therapy must be investigated in some detail, with careful attention paid to both the scientific evidence and the spiritual beliefs underlying them. We must be especially wary when supporting evidence is lacking or when evil spirits may be involved. Society should continue to seek alternatives or improvements to existing conventional medicine, but they, like any other therapy, must undergo scrutiny to ensure that they are safe and effective.

While alternative therapies offer health to those in need, they also offer answers to spiritual questions. As one seeker of health said, "I got more from mind–body medicine than I bargained for: I got religion."[67] When that religion is not Christianity, the extra bargain that comes along with the possible physical satisfaction is more costly than one could ever imagine at the time. What does it profit me if I gain the whole world and lose my soul (see Luke 17:33)? As such we must be discerning about their teachings. We must be motivated to learn more about them so we can evaluate them fairly and intelligently. We must discuss them sensitively, knowing that people often turn to them in pain and frustration. But we must also be willing to sacrifice our comfort and sometimes our health for the sake of the gospel. We must be willing to say no to some therapies, even though they might make us feel better. We must trust that Jesus Christ is the source of the true health and comfort everyone seeks. He is the true alternative to the pains and sufferings in this world.

Recommended Resources

The Center for Bioethics and Human Dignity Resources:

Kilner, John F. et al., eds., *The Changing Face of Health Care: A Christian Appraisal of Managed Care, Resource Allocation, and Patient-Caregiver Relationships*. Grand Rapids and Carlisle: Eerdmans and Paternoster, 1998.

O'Mathúna, Dónal. *Emerging Alternative/Complementary Therapies*. Available in audio and video formats.

O'Mathúna, Dónal. *Therapeutic Touch: Ethical and Theological Concerns*. Available in audio format.

Other Resources

Ankerburg, John, and John Weldon. *Can You Trust Your Doctor?* Brentwood, Tenn.: Wolgemuth & Hyatt, 1991.

Cassileth, Barrie R. *The Alternative Medicine Handbook*. New York: Norton, 1998.

Raso, Jack. "Alternative Healthcare": A Comprehensive Guide. Amherst, N.Y.: Prometheus, 1994.

Endnotes

1. Michele Blecher, "Gold in Goldenseal," *Hospitals & Health Networks* 71, no. 20 (October 1997): 50–52.

2. World Health Organization Constitution at http://who-hq-policy.who.ch/cgi-bin/folioisa.dll/basicdoc/doc

3. Michael L. Brown, *Israel's Divine Healer* (Grand Rapids: Zondervan, 1995).

4. Jacqueline Fawcett et al., "Use of Alternative Health Therapies by People with Multiple Sclerosis," *Holistic Nurse Practice* 8 (1994): 36–42.

5. Decision Resources Report, "Self Treatment in Managed Care: HMO Involvement in OTC and Alternative Therapies," cited in Jan Goodwin, "A Health Insurance Revolution," *New Age Journal* (March/April 1997): 95–99.

6. Gareth J. Daniels and Pauline McCabe, "Nursing Diagnosis and Natural Therapies: A Symbiotic Relationship," *Journal of Holistic Nursing* 12 (June 1994): 184–92.

7. Dónal P. O'Mathúna, "Emerging Alternative Therapies," in *The Changing Face of Health Care: A Christian Appraisal,* ed. John Kilner, Robert Orr, and Judy Shelly (Grand Rapids: Eerdmans, 1998).

8. Blecher, "Gold in Goldenseal," 50–52.

9. Decision Resources Report, 97.

10. David O. Weber, "The Mainstreaming of Alternative Medicine," *Healthcare Forum Journal* 39, no. 6 (November/December 1996): 16–27.

11. Goodwin, "A Health Insurance Revolution," 99.

12. Walter A. Brown, "The Placebo Effect," *Scientific American* (January 1998): 90–95.

13. Blecher, "Gold in Goldenseal, 50–52.

14. Geoffrey Cowley, "Herbal Warning: Health-Food Stores Have Built a New Natural-Drug Culture. How Safe Are Their Wares?" *Newsweek,* 6 May 1996, 60–68.
15. Hassan Rifaat, "Integrating Alternative Medicine and Managed Care," National Managed Health Care Conference, 4 April 1997, audiocassette #320-S3B.
16. Deborah A. Grandinetti, "'Integrated Medicine' Could Boost Your Income," *Medical Economics* 74, no. 18 (September 1997): 73–99.
17. http://wwwnaturopathic.org/licensingquestion. html; accessed 22 May 1998.
18. "Herbal Roulette," *Consumer Reports,* November 1995, 698–705.
19. Joseph Jacobs, quoted in Eliot Marshall, "The Politics of Alternative Medicine," *Science* 265 (September 30, 1994): 2000–02.
20. Ibid., 2002.
21. John Robbins, *Reclaiming Our Health: Exploding the Medical Myth and Embracing the Source of True Healing* (Tiburon, Calif.: H. J. Kramer, 1996), 193.
22. EEOC Compliance Manual, sec. 628: Policy guidance on "new age" training programs that conflict with employees' religious beliefs. Number N-915.022, dated September 2, 1988. Interestingly, it was signed by Clarence Thomas before his Supreme Court appointment.
23. John Robbins, *Reclaiming Our Health,* 192.
24. US Congress, Office of Technology Assessment, *Assessing the Efficacy and Safety of Medical Technologies* (Washington, D.C., 1978).
25. Kerr L. White, "Evidence-based medicine," *Lancet* 346 (September 1995): 837–8.
26. Jonathan Ellis, Ian Mulligan, James Rowe, and David L. Sackett, "Inpatient general medicine is evidence-based," *Lancet* 346 (August 1995): 407–10.
27. Russell Chandler, *Understanding the New Age* (Dallas: Word, 1988).

28. Elise Pettus, "The Mind–Body Problems," *New York*, 14 August 1995, 28–31, 95.

29. Dónal P. O'Mathúna, "Therapeutic Touch: What Could Be the Harm?" *Scientific Review of Alternative Medicine* 1, no. 2 (1998).

30. Dick Thompson, "Acupuncture Works," *Time*, 17 November 1997: NIH Consensus Statement Online: Acupuncture. 1997 November 3–5; 15, no. 5: in press. Available at http://odp.od.nih.gov/consensus/statements/cdc/107/107_stmt.html

31. Andrew A. Skolnick, "Maharishi Ayur-Veda: Guru's Marketing Scheme Promises the World Eternal 'Perfect Health,'" *Journal of the American Medical Association* 266 (October 1991): 1742.

32. Hari M. Sharma, Brihaspati Dev Triguna, and Deepak Chopra, "Maharishi Ayur-Veda: Modern Insights Into Ancient Medicine," *Journal of the American Medical Association* 265 (May 1991): 2633–5.

33. Wallace Sampson, "The Pharmacology of Chelation Therapy," *Scientific Review of Alternative Medicine* 1, no. 1 (fall/winter 1997): 23–25.

34. Joseph Weber and Sandra Dallas, "Cure? Well . . . Profit? Sure," *Business Week*, 23 October 1995, 58–59.

35. Wendy Cole and D. Blake Hallanan, "Is Homeop-athy Good Medicine?" *Time*, 25 September 1995, 47–48.

36. John Walton, Jeremiah A. Barondess, and Stephen Lock, eds., "Homoeopathy," in *The Oxford Medical Companion* (New York: Oxford University Press, 1994), 375.

37. Dana Ullman, *Discovering Homeopathy*, rev. ed. (Berkeley, Calif.: North Atlantic, 1991), 15.

38. Leon S. Otis, "Adverse Effects of Transcendental Meditation," in *Meditation: Classic and Contemporary Perspectives*, ed. Deane H. Shapiro Jr. and Roger N. Walsh (New York: Aldone, 1984), 201–07.

39. Deane H. Shapiro Jr., "Adverse Effects of Meditation: A Preliminary Investigation of Long-Term Meditators,"

International Journal of Psychosomatics 29 (1992): 62–6; Frederick J. Heide, "Relaxation: The Storm Before the Calm," *Psychology Today* (April 1985): 18–19.

40. For further information, contact the American Association of Naturopathic Physicians, 601 Valley Street, Seattle, WA 98109 at (206) 298-0126.

41. John F. Peppin, "The Osteopathic Distinction: Fact or Fiction?" *Journal of Medical Humanities* 14, no. 4 (1993): 203–22.

42. Diane Stein, *Essential Reiki* (Freedom, Calif.: Crossing Press, 1995).

43. Lynn McCutcheon, "Taking a Bite out of Shark Cartilage," *Skeptical Inquirer* 21, no. 5 (September/October 1997): 44–48.

44. Dolores Krieger, *Accepting Your Power to Heal* (Santa Fe, N.M.: Bear & Company, 1993), 29.

45. Dónal P. O'Mathúna, "The Subtle Allure of Therapeutic Touch," *Journal of Christian Nursing* 15 (winter 1998): 4–13.

46. O'Mathúna, "Therapeutic Touch: What Could Be the Harm?"

47. Krieger, *Accepting Your Power to Heal,* 20–22.

48. Shakya Zangpo and Georg Feuerstein, "The Risks of Visualization: Growing Roots Can Be Dangerous," *The Quest* (summer 1995): 26–31, 84.

49. Jonathan Adolph, "The New Age Is Now: Twenty Ideas, Books, and Records that have Redefined Our Culture," *New Age Journal* (1995 Supplement): 27–40.

50. A. A. Macdonell, "Vedic Religion," *Encyclopedia of Religion and Ethics* (Edinburgh: T & T Clark, 1955), 12:602.

51. Alice A. Bailey, *A Treatise on White Magic,* 6th ed. (New York: Lucis, 1963), 578.

52. Janet Farrar and Stewart Farrar, *A Witches Bible Compleat: Volume 2: The Rituals* (New York: Magickal Childe, 1981), 220.

53. A. E. Powell, *The Etheric Double: The Health Aura of Man* (1925; reprint: Wheaton, Ill.: Theosophical Publishing House, 1969), 74.

54. O'Mathúna, "The Subtle Allure," 4–13.

55. Malcolm Hulke, ed., "Spiritual Healing," in *The Encyclopedia of Alternative Medicine and Self-Help* (New York: Schocken Books, 1979), 178.

56. Robert Calvert, "Dolores Krieger, Ph.D. and Her Therapeutic Touch," *Massage* 47 (January/February 1994): 56–60.

57. Dolores Krieger, *The Therapeutic Touch* (Engle-wood Cliffs, N.J.: Prentice-Hall, 1979), 80.

58. Dolores Krieger, *Living The Therapeutic Touch* (New York: Dodd, Mead & Company, 1987), 53.

59. *On Christian Doctrine*, 2.45.

60. *Contra Celsum*, 3.7555.

61. *Homily 8 on Colossians*.

62. Alice A. Bailey, *A Treatise on White Magic*, 570.

63. Deborah Cowens, *A Gift for Healing: How You Can Use Therapeutic Touch* (New York: Crown Trade Paperbacks, 1996), 20.

64. A. J. Watkins and W. S. Bickel, "A Study of the Kirlian Effect," *Skeptical Inquirer* 10 (1986): 244–57.

65. Randolph C. Byrd, "Positive Therapeutic Effects of Intercessory Prayer in a Coronary Care Unit Population," *Southern Medical Journal* 81, no. 7 (July 1988): 826–29.

66. Darrel W. Amundsen and Gary B. Ferngren, "Medicine and Religion: Pre-Christian Antiquity," in *Health/Medicine and the Faith Traditions: An Inquiry into Religion and Medicine,* ed. Martin E. Marty and Kenneth L. Vaux (Philadelphia: Fortress, 1982), 53–92.

67. Marty Kaplan, "Ambushed by Spirituality," *Time,* 24 June 1996, 62.